Smartass Answers to Dumbass Questions
A Spoofbook on Everything
Leah Carson

Published by Excellent Words, LLC

This is a work of satire. Attempts to follow its mock instructions will make you crazy, although probably not as crazy as the author, who's been at it much longer than you.

ISBN 978-0-9836412-7-8

For information, contact:
Excellent Words, LLC
P.O. Box 253
Dousman WI 53118

Front and back cover photos copyright iStockphoto.com
Book design by Michael Campbell, MC Writing Services

Visit our website at www.carsonmania.com

SMARTASS ANSWERS

~ to ~

DUMBASS QUESTIONS

A Spoofbook on Everything

LEAH CARSON

DUMBASS QUESTIONS? SMARTASS ANSWERS!

We've all heard the saying "There are no stupid questions, just ignorant mistakes, so go ahead and ask."

But that's wrong. There are millions of dumbass questions. And they're just begging for smartass answers.

The questions begin in childhood. When we screw up right after being warned about something, Mom asks: "What did I just tell you?" *Gee, Mom, you can't expect me to know when you don't even remember.*

As teens, we ask whiny questions:

"Why do I always get stuck loading the dishwasher?"
Because it would literally kill you to hand-wash this pile of dishes.

"Do I have to take English 101?"
Well, since you're the only student clever enough to ask, we'll let you take Nudes in Renaissance Art instead.

As adults, we ask questions at home:

"Can't we ever have a little peace and quiet around here?"
No.

"All right, who broke the lamp?"
Hint: it wasn't the dog.

"Where the heck are my reading glasses?"
Umm, on top of your head.

Then other people ask us questions, like at the supermarket checkout:

"Did you find everything you were looking for?"
No, but let's hold up the line while you page a clerk who won't find it, either.

Or at the hardware store:

"Would you like a bag for that?"
Naw, I'd rather balance this can of paint and five rolls of duct tape on my head.

Or strolling down the sidewalk:

"Ooh, is this your doggie?!"
No, it's our kid, going through an ugly stage.

And that's just the beginning…

CONTENTS

Carson's Final Eleven: Read These When You Have Nothing Better to Do

CARSON'S ELEVEN: THE FUNNIEST CHAPTERS EVER WRITTEN

DEAR DUMB HOUSEHOLD HINTS

Dear Dumb Household Hints: Sometimes our local grocery store offers "two for one" sales on frozen foods, but I can't take advantage of these low prices because my freezer drawer is already full. *— Struggling in Cincinnati*

Dear Struggling: That's terrible! No one should have to pass up a bargain due to lack of freezer space. I contacted the head of customer relations at the national headquarters of your supermarket. He suggested that you buy a deep freezer. Those hulking appliances used to be very popular until consumers realized they were paying an extra $200 per month on their electric utility bill. The good news is that some manufacturers still offer brand-new deep freezers, and you can find used ones at estate sales and county landfills. Once your deep freezer is installed in the garage, you can save 50 cents or even 75 cents on those frozen-food sales every week. Happy shopping!

Dear Dumb Household Hints: Here's a fun project. Wash an empty margarine tub and drill a hole in the center. Turn it bottom-side up and insert a used Popsicle stick, then glue a cotton ball on top. Spray-paint the whole thing with seasonal colors, like red and green for Christmas, or orange and black for Halloween. Finally, use a caulk gun to add eyes, nose and mouth to the cotton ball head. *— Cheapo Crafter*

Dear Cheapo: I'm gladly printing your letter, because Cotton Stick Man is my readers' favorite craft. Every week I get hundreds of letters like yours, many with clever variations:

- My family doesn't like Popsicles, so I asked our doctor's office to save used tongue depressors for me.
- I lined up four stick figures on the left, four on the right, and a tall one in the middle, and voila!… I've created a menorah. If a Jewish family ever moves into our neighborhood, this will be the perfect housewarming gift.
- Our kids name their Cotton Stick Men after classmates they don't like, then set them on fire.

Dear Dumb Household Hints: When our eldest daughter got married, the florist accidentally included poison ivy in her bouquet. She broke into a rash so severe that we had to cancel the reception. Luckily, the reception hall and the caterer refunded our payments, which we later spent on a Caribbean cruise. Should we ask the florist to create another poison ivy bouquet when our youngest daughter gets married next month? She and her fiancé booked a really expensive country club. — *Mom & Dad Who Can't Say No*

Dear Can't Say No: Two poison ivy incidents in a row would look pretty suspicious, so I asked professional wedding planners to describe wedding day disasters that prompted refunds. Here are a few: "A hurricane flattened the supper club. Five years later, FEMA refunded the parents' down payment." "Potato salad with mayonnaise sent dozens of guests to the emergency room with food poisoning; the caterer reimbursed the bride and groom 5% of the buffet charge." "The bride's brother, an angry Mafioso, broke the photographer's camera and tossed $50 bills at his feet." I realize these aren't exactly the "easy out" you were looking for. You might have better luck telling the country club (and your daughter) that you're about to declare bankruptcy and the bank is foreclosing on your mortgage. If everyone believes you, rent a barn for a simple country-style wedding.

Dear Dumb Household Hints: Some time ago, you offered a recipe for Manwich Sandwich, but I've misplaced it. Could you please publish the recipe again? — *Recipeless*

Dear Recipeless: Of course! Simply add one can of Manwich sauce to one pound cooked ground beef. And don't forget to rinse out the empty Manwich can and keep it on your kitchen counter. The recipe is printed right there on the label. Bon appetit!

Dear Dumb Household Hints: I make jewelry from beads and baubles, but it's hard to keep those tiny pieces from rolling around and getting lost. I found the perfect solution at the dollar store: plastic ice cube trays. Each tray corrals beads of similar sizes and colors. — *Wise Wife*

Dear Dumb Household Hints: After our automatic icemaker broke, we were spending a fortune on bags of ice from the liquor store. Then it hit me: my wife's jewelry storage containers were the perfect size for making ice. I dumped all the beads into a cardboard box, filled the plastic trays with water, and froze a batch of perfect ice cubes. — *Wise Guy*

Dear Dumb Household Hints: For years, I've been wrapping gifts with brown grocery bags and newspaper comic sections, as you often suggest. But the paper bags made it look like my gifts came from Publix, and newsprint rubbed off on fingers and clothing. Then, this week, I saw a new product at Walmart: wrapping paper! It comes in dozens of colors and themes. You just roll out a length, cut it, and wrap it around the present. They also sell bows! I used to have the darndest time making bows out of newspaper. — *All Wrapped Up*

Dear All Wrapped Up: I'm happy to share your tip. Other readers have told me about gift *bags,* which are even easier to use. I imagine that someday we'll be able to buy matching gift tags, too. When these come on the market, I'll be sure to announce it in my column.

Dear Dumb Household Hints: I've tried many ways to seal a jug of milk: rubber bands over plastic wrap; aluminum foil; parchment paper; and masking tape. The best method is to use the cap that comes with the

bottle. Whenever I want milk, I twist off the cap, pour the milk, then twist the cap back on again. Works every time! — *Milk Man*

Dear Milk Man: Thanks for another clever hint that I'm pleased to pass along to everyone.

Dear Readers: Zipper stuck? Try rubbing a candle along it — but if it's the zipper in your trouser fly, don't do this in public. Maybe you don't have any candles lying around, in which case you could try rubbing with a piece of hard cheese like Parmesan, Romano, or vintage Gouda. WD-40 might also work, though I haven't tried it.

Dear Readers: My recent column "Weird Uses for Ordinary Household Items" prompted a deluge of mail. Here are many of the clever ideas you provided.

- Baby wipes: Disinfecting surgical instruments
- Surgical wipes: Disinfecting babies' butts
- Empty pods from Keurig Coffee Machine: On-the-go spittoons
- Pantyhose: Are you kidding? Who owns pantyhose anymore?
- Plastic gallon milk jugs: Nail together to make a Christmas lawn ornament that looks just like a snowman made of empty gallon milk jugs
- Toothpaste: Seal grout around window exteriors
- Women's size 42 DDD-cup bra: Fill one cup with birdseed, the other with water, and hang in the garden as a one-stop feeding station for wild birds

ASK THE PET PSYCHIC

By guest columnist Rona Ronaditsy

My new cat, Doris, meows constantly, bullies my other cats, and won't play with her toys. I can't seem to please her. Is this typical Siamese cat behavior?

I spoke at length with Doris about her previous life as Cleopatra, Queen of the Nile. Understandably, she regards her current situation as a bit of a letdown. You can get back into her good graces by fulfilling these demands: (1) Rather than "Doris," address her as Most Royal and Exalted Queen; (2) fill her bowl with wild-caught Atlantic salmon twice a day; and (3) provide a team of white mice to bear her upon a litter from room to room, from pillow to windowsill, and from scratching post to the silk damask chair in the foyer.

Bowser, our bulldog, keeps peeing on our Oriental rug. What's up with that?

He thinks the rug is ugly. And he's right! Get rid of it! Shop online for a replacement, and get Bowser's approval before you click "Add to cart."

Why does our dog Rufus lick his privates all the time?

He's trying to freshen his breath.

Last year I bought a mated pair of adorable teddy-bear hamsters. As far as I can tell, Bob and Bonnie haven't mated yet. I was really looking

forward to a litter of these cuties. I've tried bribes (promises of fresh dandelion stems), threats (warning to take away their exercise wheel), and reverse psychology ("Who needs kids, anyway, when there's so much more to life?") Nothing works.

When I communicated via long-distance telepathy with your hamsters, they made it clear that "Bonnie" is actually "Brian." But don't give up on your dream of a litter; the guys told me they'd love to raise a family. You just need to find young-ish hamsters so that Bob & Brian (and you!) can experience the pitter patter of little paws around the cage. Skip the bargain pet store that sold you B&B. Instead, adopt pups from a reputable private breeder who can tell a "boar" from a "sow" hamster. As a first-time stepmom, you should ask the private breeder for all-male pups, unless you're prepared to raise several dozen litters within the next month.

Where's my boa constrictor?! The kids left the top of Butch's cage wide open, and now he's gone. I'm not worried about my kids — they can probably break his stranglehold — but I don't want our cat Fluffy to wind up as the proverbial bulge in Butch's middle.

I spent a few hours communing with the old skin you sent me from Butch's last shedding cycle. It positively vibrated with longing for the open sea. Assuming Butch hasn't left your house, check your bathtub, leaky pipes beneath sinks, and the basement sump pump. Meanwhile, lock Fluffy in a room without any plumbing fixtures.

My bottlenose dolphin stole my identity and left town. Now my credit score is ruined, creditors are constantly harassing me, and I'm afraid to drive because he also took my license. Flipper used to be such a good boy. I'm heartbroken — and broke, period.

I'm sorry to hear of your situation. Bottlenose dolphins usually are very amiable and trustworthy. While viewing Flipper's photo, I discerned that he was living in Las Vegas — truly an odd choice for someone of his breed. I couldn't feel any further vibes, so I texted him using the number of your missing cellphone. It's a good thing I speak Dolphinese, because Flipper promptly called me back and practically *chit-chit-chitted* my ear off. The upshot: He hates being called Flipper. That cliché name is the equivalent of Lassie for a collie or Bugs Bunny for a rabbit. The Dolphin Formerly Known as Flipper has agreed to come home if you promise to call him George. I'll put you in touch with a skilled aquatic-family counselor so the two of you can re-establish trust and affection. Good luck!

Our Shih Tzu wants to herd cattle, but she's just not cut out for the job. Her heart is set on this. How can we let her down gently?

Before you redirect Little Miss Shitz to a more suitable career, indulge her dream by sending her to fantasy herding camp. Seasoned cowpokes lead their canine campers in a roundup of slow-moving, dimwitted creatures such as water buffalo, sloths, and snails. Once your Shih Tzu gets that herding mania out of her system, she'll happily settle into her groove as lap dog, couch potato, cuddle bug, and floor mop.

I'm trying to "tidy" our home aquariums and put everybody in one tank. Can a Torpedo Shark coexist with guppies?

Yes, for about 30 seconds.

My landlord is threatening eviction because my cat, Zsa Zsa, has started clawing the woodwork whenever I'm not there to "redirect" her with a quick spritz from a water bottle. I've tried locking her in the bathroom when I'm about to leave, but she screams bloody murder.

You're in luck. Zsa Zsa is simply jealous that you get manicures and she doesn't. You can pamper her with a spa-worthy nail treatment without leaving home. "Nail caps" for cats come in many colors, including Purple Feather Teaser, Catnip Green, Hairball Grey and Mangled Mouse Red. Zsa Zsa is actually quite laid-back when she's not in solitary confinement, and she told me she wants Litterbox Beige nails. Oh, and lay off the water spritzer for a while. How would you like it if someone blasted you with a fire hose whenever you got out of line?

Our pet giraffes, Harold and Maude, have expressed interest in becoming therapy animals. I'm not so sure. Could we make this work?

Absolutely! Your giraffes told me they want to greet people in hospitals, nursing homes, schools and minimum-security prisons. This isn't as impractical as you might think. Harold and Maude explained that they can interact with any humans standing near an open window on the second or third floor. Even a prison meet-and-greet should be okay; just clear it with the warden so nobody gets shot leaning through a barred window to pet them. Take it from me: jaded people who are bored with visits from therapy dogs and therapy cats will perk up at the sight of a giraffe's skyscraper neck, ossicones (antlers), and weird blue tongue.

As a new rabbit owner, I was told to place their meal of hay at one end of their litterbox, since rabbits tend to eat and poop at the same time! What are my rabbits thinking when they do this?

I zoned in on their little rabbit brains and got different answers from each.

Harriet:
"Hay creates an endless loop.
The more I eat, the more I poop.
The more I poop, the better I feel,
So let's have hay at every meal!"

Earl:
"Nice to get everything done in one go."

Trinket:
"Mmmm, tasty hay! [munch, munch]...Um, what's going on back there? [munch, munch]...Why does this cafeteria always smell like a restroom?"

Before I adopted an African pygmy hedgehog, I knew he would be shy at first. Sure enough, little Norton curled up into a ball in the palm of my hand. He hadn't uncurled by bedtime, so I placed him in a safe spot on the kitchen counter. That was four days ago, and he's still sitting there in a spiky ball.

When you FaceTimed me, the answer became clear at once. Norton has indeed uncurled and is waiting to bond with you. He's the porcupine-ish critter with the adorable nose and ears, sitting behind the bottle of Dawn dishwashing liquid. That other "spiky ball" you've been fretting over is a metal pot scrubber.

NOW HEAR THIS! IMPORTANT STUFF WE WANT THE WORLD TO KNOW

Good morning, listeners, and welcome to "Now Hear This!" Each week we connect people who have urgent messages — or at least they *think* they're urgent — with people who urgently need to hear them. I'm Brad Glibman, ready to share your message with the world.

Our first caller is Kip Kiprakip of Kenya. Kip, welcome to the show. What's on your mind?

I have a very important message, a vital message for the world. Every week these ladies send us quilts. Always the quilts they send to our village of Gumwad.

Women send you quilts?

Yes, these are ladies from the United States of America who make the quilts by hand. Then they send them to us. Dozens of quilts each time. They send for charity.

And what is your message for the quilters, Kip?

Stop sending these quilts! In our village, it is hot every day. We wear light clothing and use the fan whenever electrical power is on. We

certainly do not need quilts! These ladies write notes saying they
work together on the quilts every week, and they know their sewing
goes for a good cause. But not here!

How did these ladies learn of your village?

I have not the slightest idea! Every quilt package does not have a
proper return address — it says only "The Quilting Angels of Sinkhole
Acres, Florida." We carry the quilts to the farthest edge of our village,
but the pile is now so big it blocks the wind. Please, someone tell
these ladies not to send any more quilts!

**Thank you for your call, Kip. Okay, listeners, if anyone knows these
"quilting angels," tell them to send their quilts somewhere else, like
maybe Uganda, ha ha ha!**

Next up is Greta Fatterumpf of Munich. What's on your mind, Greta?

Guten Morgen, Herr Glibman. Mein urgent message is about Oktoberfest in Munich. People coming here from the United States have und
mistake in their heads, und we must correct it.

OK, Greta, so what's their mistaken impression?

They think Oktoberfest is in October.

Um, yeahhhh...?

But we hold Oktoberfest in September!

Whaaaat?

Ya, das ist der Oktoberfest, in September. Und when Americans come
to Munich in der middle of October, all das beer is gone, der festival
tents are gone, und even die gemutlichkeit is gone. We are all pooped.

Those tourists must be royally ticked off.

Ya! They want to drink beer from big steins. They want to sit in big
tents and sing "Ein Prosit." They want to see waitresses in peasant
blouses that show off their big Deutsche Bruste.

I hope the FCC doesn't fine us for that remark. But thank you for calling, Greta.

Our next caller, Logan Mildguy, lives in Borington, Manitoba, Canada. What's up, Logan?

Yeah, Brad, I hate to pile on, but my message is for the United States, too.

Today must be Pick on Uncle Sam Day! Tell us your message, Logan.

Here in Canada, we have a reputation for being nice. Too nice, actually. Some people take it as a challenge. They try to goad us into being not-nice.

Aw, I bet they're just kidding around.

Yeah, that's what they say, and then they really turn up the heat. Last week, some guys from Detroit who came here to go fly-fishing started razzing me about my toque.

Your what?

My wool hat. You know, a beanie hat. It's red knit with a pompom on top.

Oh yeah, I've seen those. Dorky!

I beg your pardon?

C'mon, Logan, those hats make a guy look like Napoleon Dynamite of the Northwoods.

Hmmph. This is exactly what I'm talking about! I have to warn you, I'm feeling very uncharitable right now.

Logan, buddy, chill out! Just because you wear a silly hat —

All right, that's it! Now the gloves are coming off!

Don't you mean the dorky red mittens are coming off?

Grrrr. You, Brad, you're just — just a…bad egg! There, I said it!

A "bad egg"?! That's hysterical!

No, it's not. I really mean it. You're a bad egg, and you'd better not visit us. Everyone in Borington listens to your show, and if you come here, nobody will smile at you! Not the tour guides! Not the canoe rental people! Not even the ladies at the tourist information center!

Oooh. I'm quaking in my waders! Well, folks, we're out of time. Tune in next week for a special edition, "Now Hear This! Messages from Outer Space." So long!

DEATH BY PICKLEBALL: YOUR HYPERACTIVE RETIREMENT YEARS

What's this "pickleball" everyone's yammering about?

Ah, yes. You must be approaching retirement. The moment you turn 60, your email in-box is flooded with videos of abnormally cheerful players: "Pickleball: a funny name for a fun game!" and "What's pickleball? (long pause) Well, it's like…it's similar to…gosh, it's hard to say!"

Later, these messages turn serious. "Pickleball saved our marriage." "My hair grew in again, thanks to pickleball." "Pickleball tournaments have brought peace to the Middle East."

So here's what they're yammering about: pickleball combines elements of tennis, badminton, ping pong, and whacking a piñata, but it's much easier because you're using a 3-foot-wide paddle on a court that's smaller than a queen bed. Also, the top of the net is just 6 inches off the ground.

Who, me play pickleball?

You'll know you're ready for retirement when pickleball seems like a good idea. If that doesn't happen by the time you turn 65, the Pickleball Mafia sends Luca Brasi to your house. He assures you that either your brains or your signature will be on the sign-up form for Pickleball 101.

Bring this equipment to your first lesson:

- beginner's racket made of Styrofoam, balsa wood, or cardboard
- a perforated polymer ball similar to a Whiffle Ball, but with much less Whiffle

You'll need special shoes that provide support for side-to-side movement. Unlike bowling alleys, pickleball courts don't offer shoes for rent, so beg, borrow or steal a pair for your first lesson. Come dressed in your most comfortable gear; just about anything goes, including kilts and pajamas.

Competitive player matchups include:

- one on one
- two on two
- two on one, if "one's" partner is in the hospital having open-heart surgery
- four on eleven when relatives from up north are visiting
- one-half on one when "one-half" had a knee replaced yesterday

Just as in tennis, pickleball prohibits these "faults":

- greasing the ball with lard
- texting during the match
- shouting "Geronimo!" as you serve
- smashing the ball into your opponent's face
- jumping over the net to shake hands with your opponent before the match is over

Pickleball sounds like too much work. I'd like something more relaxing. Am I too old for pot?

Never! Consider these two facts: Most Florida retirees are extremely friendly and mellow — and medical marijuana is legal in Florida. Coincidence?

While it's true that pot can leave you dazed, confused, slack-jawed, and wandering around in circles, you already act like this at retirement age, so you might as well feel groovy, too.

Hey, Baby Boomers, remember your college years? So much pot smoking took place in the "supervised" freshman dorms that we had to visit local taverns just to clear our lungs. But now that ordinary smoking is a social kiss of death, licensed marijuana dispensaries offer many alternatives:

- eyedroppers that deliver tincture oil under your tongue or inside your armpit
- spray bottles for that amazing "stoned tonsils" vibe
- softgel tablets for discreet zoning when you're out with friends; everybody takes so many medications that they won't even notice yours
- transdermal patches that deliver concentrated relief to any point on your body — for occasions when your bald spot needs to mellow out

I can't drive more than a block in Florida without seeing billboards for "active retirement" developments. What's that all about?

An active retirement community is a wonderful place to stay constantly on the go-go-go until the moment you're dead and gone-gone-gone. To meet community covenants, at least one member of the household must be age 55-plus and look good in a golf outfit.

You'll expand your cultural horizons by meeting scores of rich white Republicans who cruise around in golf carts with their itty-bitty foo-foo dogs. As time goes on, you'll discern subtle differences that make each resident unique. Some play beginners' pickleball, while others play expert pickleball. Some dress their foo-foo dogs in different outfits each week; others save the dress-ups for major holidays. Some went to see Gary Lewis and the Playboys at the entertainment center Thursday night, while others wish they'd gone because their friends raved about the show. Some enjoy Sunday brunch at the country club, especially the key lime pie; others enjoy Sunday brunch at the country club, especially the banana cream pie.

People are so ramped up about "The Villages" that it sounds like a cult. Is this for real?

It's not just real, it's surreal. Here's a brief overview.

The Villages is a planned community in central Florida designed for hyperactive, hyper-social seniors determined to "play that funky music till you die."

The population of The Villages stood at 578 million at the end of last year and continues to increase by more than 79,000 per month.

The Villages' pickleball courts are visible from outer space.

Of the 489 homeowners who move to The Villages each day, 90% come from other parts of Florida without enough pickleball courts. The rest are from New Jersey.

Florida has alligators in every body of water bigger than a toilet bowl. The Villages' alligators kept a low profile until one 15-footer ("Larry") was caught on video sauntering down the golf cart path. Despite his commercial value of $25,000 as a handbag, The Villages did the right thing by relocating Larry to a gator refuge.

The Villages and surrounding communities offer houses of worship for every major faith and even some minor ones, like the St. Vincent de Lombardi Society; You're All Doomed (Minnesota Synod); The Divine Order of Fries; Fallen-Away Cat People; and our favorite, the

Frisbeeterians, who believe that when you die, your soul flies up on the roof and gets stuck there.

As you'd expect among retirees, most services are packed with grey- and white-haired worshippers. The good news: there aren't any long-winded children's sermons or baptisms. The bad news: so many parishioners fall asleep during the homily that the priest blesses everybody with a Super Soaker filled with holy water.

What else is different about religious practices?

Everything happens before dark, because everybody goes to bed early. The Christmas Eve midnight Mass begins at 5 p.m. One year during Lent, several churches co-hosted a live tableau of the Last Supper — but since they couldn't get enough volunteers for an evening performance, they staged the Last Brunch instead. Thousands of people came to view it, on the mistaken impression that free lunch was available.

Church councils of elders are reeeealllly elders. Some of them knew Jesus personally, although they're a little fuzzy on the details, and anyway they'd rather talk about Gary Lewis and the Playboys.

What about other mainstream religions: Jewish, Hindu, Muslim, Buddhist?

We're too lazy to visit every single denomination. If you're interested, just show up for worship and hope for the best. They're always happy for new blood, assuming you have any.

What should I consider when home-shopping in The Villages?

Besides checking for typical Florida issues like sinkholes, huge Burmese pythons, alligators, termites, and garish flamingo wallpaper, consider these aspects of Villages life:

Is the home within golf-cart distance of the hottest pickup joints (for him) and mah-jongg clubs (for her)? Will you be close enough to enjoy nightly live music at the town square? Is the house so close to the town square that your dentures rattle when the bass player cranks up the volume? Does Papa John's deliver pizza in your area? If you don't like Papa John's, why are you wondering how close they are?

Yet all this nitpicking is irrelevant in a hot real estate market. In that case, you must be the first buyer through the door with a wheelbarrow full of cash.

But what if you can't be there in person because you're still working at a job you hate and your Ebenezer Scrooge boss won't give you time off? Never fear, the buyer's agent is here. This expert in "remote sales" makes the offer for you, with specially minted gold bars that will dazzle the sellers. The agent also gives you a virtual tour using FaceTime on her iPad, so you won't be too shocked by the orange shag carpeting and the maroon walls when you finally get a chance to visit your new old house.

I thought I'd spend retirement watching TV and taking long naps. Do I really need to get involved in group activities?

Haven't you heard all the media hype about social interaction? Socializing with others postpones the onset of dementia for at least five days, injects "good" bacteria into your gut, and helps you remember where you parked the car. So take advantage of a few dozen activities offered in your community.

Warning for introverts: Don't count on blending in with the wallpaper like you usually do. You will be forced to make eye contact. Expect some buttinski questions. How you answer them is your own business, but keep in mind that juicy items have a half-life of 7,000 years through the grapevine.

Warning for extroverts: We know you're only there for the gabfest, but at least pretend to be interested. Read the front and back covers of the novel your book club chose this month. If you want to join the Cavalier King Charles Spaniel Owners Group, borrow a dog, or bring a picture of one. Arrive with some yarn and at least one knitting needle for your We Luv Potholders club.

And now, let's look at a bunch of activities offered by The Villages and other mega-retirement communities.

Painting On Your Own

Only in a retirement community could painting "on your own" become a group activity. It doesn't take much to stand out in such a class. You might be the only one who's painting, while the others catch up on neighborhood news. Introverts: if you desperately want to be left alone, paint a weird abstract that looks like a Rorschach inkblot test.

Rock Painting

So simple! So carefree! You and a bunch of other ladies get together and…paint rocks. And talk, of course. Talk about which rocks are best for rock painting. Which paints are best for rock painting. Whether you should wear an artist's smock while painting your rocks.

After you've painted 20 or 30 rocks, talk about what you're going to do with them. Give them to your grandchildren, who will cherish them forever. Give them to your friends, to be displayed prominently on the fireplace mantel. Leave a box of rocks at a neighbor's front door with a "secret Santa" note. Set a date for your class to host a public stoning.

Coloring for Grownups

Channel your inner 4-year-old by drawing outside the lines with crayons, felt-tip pens, charcoal, or Mom's lipstick. Then move from coloring books to more challenging media: the living room curtains, the kitchen wall, lampshades, throw pillows, and your baby sister's face.

Advanced Sketching: Drawing the Human Figure

This one's not for the faint of heart. Imagine how your classmates in "Painting On Your Own" would look posing in the nude. That image could haunt you for the rest of your life. And in all fairness, when it's your turn to pose, you'd probably clear the room.

Basket Weaving: It's Not Just for Sanitariums Anymore

Basket weaving provides an oasis of calm in the hectic retirement life-style of golf, bridge games, gardening, golf, walking the dog, and still more golf. Getting started in basket weaving is easy. Just buy a few hundred dollars' worth of weaving material such as canes, willows and spaghetti *al dente*, and spend another hundred dollars for tools like scissors, knife, round-nose pliers and Band-Aids.

Find a group of weavers with patience for beginners' questions: "Do I start at the left side or the right?" "I want to weave a replica of the Lockheed F-117 Stealth Fighter," or "My basket is getting too big. Can I shrink it in the microwave?" After a couple of years on the learning curve, you can create a basket that rivals any you'd find at Walmart for $4.99.

One little-known secret of basket weaving is a "bodkin," a pointed metal tool with a wooden handle. Buy one so you can impersonate a Shakespearean actor who repeatedly shouts "Odds bodkins!" Do it often enough and you'll get yourself kicked out of the basket weavers club, which leaves you more time for golf.

Playing weird musical instruments

Chromatic harmonica: Much larger than the familiar diatonic harmonica, this monster makes you look like you're trying to eat a radiator. Some groups allow visitors to sit in and listen, and if you're curious, they'll lend you one of their own instruments (eeewww!).

Autoharp: No, this doesn't involve autos, and it's not an idiot-proof automatic harp. The autoharp is a hollow box with strings that are strummed with a pick. Associated with avant-garde musicians like Mother Maybelle Carter, the autoharp will make you a big hit at parties. Parties with your autoharp clubmates, that is.

Hammered dulcimer: This instrument looks like somebody gutted a piano's soundboard/strings and glued them to a card table. You strike the strings with long "hammer" sticks. Whenever club members get bored (often), they host BYOB parties at which every-body gets hammered.

Cliché activities for oldies

Bocce ball: Bocce ball involves rolling small, heavy objects known as "balls" down a lane of two parallel lines known as a "court." In regulation play, the court measures 90 feet long by 30 feet wide. In a friendly match with elderly players, it's more like 30 feet long by 90 feet wide.

Shuffleboard: If you can push a lightweight pole at least six inches, you can play shuffleboard. This perennial geriatric favorite improves eye-hand coordination and gives you something to talk about, besides your ongoing medical issues. When even this becomes too strenuous, there's tabletop shuffleboard, played with checkers and toothpicks.

Corn toss: Players toss beanbags toward holes in angled boards on the ground. Most matches are BYOC (Bring Your Own Corn.) Corn toss's predecessor was the lawn game Jarts, for which "you'll shoot your eye out" wasn't just a punchline. The only danger with corn toss is accidentally beaning somebody with a beanbag. Come to think of it, they really should call them cornbags. Suggest this to the other players. Maybe they'll give you some money.

Mah-jongg: The Chinese imported this devious game to America as revenge for mistreatment of Chinese railroad workers in the 1860s. Small tiles are arranged on the table according to secret rules avail-able only to those of Chinese descent. In addition, there are regional variations, various scoring systems, and even private table rules which aren't announced until a Foreign Devil claims to have won.

Bonsai: In this classic Japanese art form, small plants are painstak-ingly crafted to look like miniature trees. Class time is divided equally between looking at everyone's trees and talking about everyone's trees. Pruning sessions with nail scissors and tweezers occur twice yearly. Potential members must commit to attending meetings every Wednesday for life.

Gratuitous World War II reference: Bonsai is not to be confused with shouts of "Banzai!!!" by Japanese suicide pilots ramming their planes into Allied naval vessels.

I'm not a golfer. Will I feel out of place in a retirement neighborhood?

You don't need to golf. Just buy a golf cart and drive it everywhere. It's a loyalty test: If you're willing to look like the Flintstones, then you're in with the in crowd. Drive it to church, Friday night fish fry, rec center games of Mexican Train Dominoes and Bingo, water aerobics at the pool, shuffleboard — and, of course, pickleball.

Isn't there any way to make my golf cart less dorky?

Some popular add-ons include:

Huge 8-foot all-terrain tires make you the biggest badass of the cart path. On the downside, you'll need a ladder to climb into the driver's seat.

A street-legal engine enables speeds of up to 50 mph. You'll take corners on two wheels and have the best bragging rights in the intensive care unit.

Underbody LED lights come in handy when that speed bump you just ran over turns out to be a neighbor.

Rear-facing extra seats let you take along several "nieces" (young, pretty gals from a local modeling agency).

Just remember: no matter how you paint, rebuild, outfit or jack up your cart, its high dome atop that flat carriage will always look ludicrous. Sometimes, aging gracelessly is the only option.

I can't decide between a gas-powered cart or an electric cart.

Mostly it's a matter of personal preference. Would you rather run out of gasoline halfway home, or forget to recharge it overnight and never leave home to begin with?

Other considerations:

- Gas carts are noisy and smelly, providing a polite distraction in public if you, too, are gassy and smelly.
- Electric carts are nearly silent when running. You can sneak up on water birds and gators.
- According to one of our (unreliable) sources, electric carts are "the clear choice for use indoors." Do they mean zipping around Walmart, or just idling in the garage? Use your best judgment.

THE LIFE-CHANGING MAGIC OF COMPULSIVELY FOLDING YOUR SOCKS

By guest columnist Maria Tatonka

I'd like to get organized, but — folding socks and underwear? Really? That's ridiculous! Can't I just pile them in the drawer?

Yes, that would be the lazy way out, but it leads to utter chaos: underwear not sorted by color, style or width, thongs scattered among old-lady white-balloon undies — or, in extreme cases, a woman's underwear mingled with her husband's boxer shorts. These "undies in a bundle" will bring dishonor upon your house. You will be forced to publicly apologize to your family, your friends, your neighbors, and your dead ancestors.

I tried folding my shirts and pants, but they don't stand up properly in the drawer.

You must show them who's boss, or soon they will spark anarchy. Say: "Look here, clothes! Straighten up and lie right! Square your edges, stiffen your zippers, and get your hems together."

Conclude this lecture with a stern glance. Then shut the drawer. The next time you peek at the wayward clothes, they should be much tidier. If not, reinforce your commands with a few hard raps from a yardstick. It may seem cruel, but a quick correction now will save you and your rebellious clothing years of grief down the road.

Ugh. Folding sounds boring.

On the contrary, folding is fun! Once you experience 20 minutes of zen while aligning every single thread of one shirt, you'll want to do it over and over. And over. And over. I get goosebumps just thinking about it.

Also, folding isn't just for clothes! You can fold so many things! Fold your pets; they'll feel soothed under compression. Fold leftovers before storing them in the refrigerator. Fold home office items like pencils, paper clips, and scissors.

While cleaning out my closet, I found seven girdles. And I'm a guy. I have no idea how they got there.

That's nothing. Here are some really weird stockpiles I've found in clients' homes:

- 16 potato peelers, including five with power attachments
- a two-car garage filled floor to ceiling with didgeridoos from the Australian outback
- 25 sets of ballet tutus, size 48XX
- a tuba marked "Return this to Grandma after the parade"
- a papier-mâché bust of Susan B. Anthony
- 17,000 weathered-wood "See Rock City" signs

My closets are OK, but piles of old photographs are taking over my home. Help!

Many people get stuck at this stage. Whenever we're sorting old photos, I bring along two bottles of Valium, one for me and one for my client.

You must locate all the photos hidden throughout your house, bring them together in a huge pile, and sort the entire mess without getting distracted by your usual daily routine. Set aside six months for this process. Take an extended leave of absence from your job and hire a maid, cook, nanny and any other professionals required to carry out your household responsibilities.

Each day, climb Mount Photo and sort for at least 18 hours. Choose one photo at a time and ask yourself: "Does this picture spark joy, boredom, rage, uncontrolled weeping, jealousy, schadenfreude, an epileptic seizure, or something else?"

Place the photos in boxes marked "Save for scrapbook," "Burn," "Useful as blackmail," "Paste on dartboard," and "Drop off at my sister's place when she's not home."

Beware of placing too many photos in the scrapbook box. A scrap-booking addiction can make the six-month photo-sorting task seem like a walk in the park.

I have trouble getting rid of things people gave me.

Don't get sentimental over junk you never wanted. If a gift doesn't suit your taste, just say "sayonara." Give it to Goodwill so it can find a happy home. You'd be amazed how many people will pay 50 cents for that green porcelain Kokopelli or the Ecuadorian peasant blouse with "Muy buena" embroidered on the bodice.

Some people hesitate to regift items to a local charity; they're afraid the original gift-giver will be crushed to see their present sitting on a store shelf. Look on the bright side: If they decide you're an ungrateful wretch, they'll stop giving you stuff.

Our guest bathroom contains 1,672 grooming items we've "liberated" from hotel rooms: scented soap, shampoo, hair conditioner, shower caps, and travel-size sewing kits. The supply never seems to dwindle.

How often do your guests stay overnight? Perhaps once a year? People who stop by for coffee rarely wash their hair or stitch a loose hem.

Next time you travel, liberate something worthwhile from the hotel, like a plush robe or a flat-panel TV. Place it in your guest room with a gift note saying "with my compliments" for those annual overnight visitors. Your reputation as a hostess with the mostess will soar.

WHY PATIENTS ARE LOSING PATIENCE

The last time I went to the doctor, he barely looked up from his laptop. My appointment lasted just 5 minutes. Should I try to find a new doctor?

That wouldn't help. They're all under the gun — so many regulations, so little time. Many physicians are switching to careers that allow more hands-on work, like shift manager at Hardee's, or pit boss at a casino.

Aren't there any doctors who'll spend more time with me?

Try this: go into cardiac arrest. If the ER isn't too busy that night, you might get 5 minutes with a doctor and, let's say, three assistants. Multiply 5 times 4, and your medical-attention score would reach a whopping 20 minutes.

I got so irritated at my annual checkup! They made me fill out several long documents that had nothing to do with my chronic allergy.

And that's not the worst of it. Once you give them the forms, the clerical staff promptly shreds them, in compliance with HIPAA regulations.

Sometimes the documents are scanned into your permanent record before shredding. Your record is uploaded to the cloud, where it is stored under the strictest privacy protocols by Facebook, Twitter, Google, Snapchat, Instagram, WhatsApp, Tinder, and the IRS.

The most widely used patient questionnaire is the Universal CYA (Cover Your Ass) Form, issued by the nation's largest legal firms on behalf of their client hospitals. We've reprinted it here so you can brace yourself before your next appointment.

UNIVERSAL CYA FORM

To the patient: Fill out each section below. If you need help, you may call a friend or relative and carry on a loud conversation in the waiting room. DO NOT take this form to the restroom and place it on the toilet tank. DO NOT doodle in the margins. DO NOT fold it into a paper airplane or an origami crane.

IDENTIFYING INFORMATION
Name:

Principal address:

Other residences, such as a second home, luxury RV, or yacht:

(This information enables our Billing Department to adjust your fee for today's office visit.)

Cellphone:

Burner phone:

Emergency contact:

(List only someone who will actually take our call — not your ex, your boss or your second cousin working on a pipeline way the heck up in Alaska.)

WHAT BRINGS YOU HERE TODAY? Circle all that apply.
Pregnancy concerns
Lunacy concerns
My wife nagged me into it

Fallen arches

Fallen dentures

Other fallen parts (specify)

Tsetse fly disease

Dandruff

Swordfight injury

Stubbed my toe

Complications of frontal lobotomy

None of your business

Pain in right dorsal fin

Raging food poisoning (Please ask for a buzzer and wait in the restroom until we summon you.)

Foot-in-mouth disease

Didn't sleep well last night

Misplaced thumb

Need referral for exorcism

I can't read the fine print on the informational insert for my prescription medicine, Placebo-tine. In fact, I don't even remember why I'm taking Placebo-tine.

We obtained the following information from the product's most recent consumer advisory.

Placebo-tine

Recommended for patients who keep bugging their doctors about imaginary ailments

Active ingredients: None.

Inactive ingredients: Table sugar, food coloring, cornstarch, dryer lint, and grit.

Contains at least 10% of the Recommended Daily Allowance of nitroglycerin.

Potential side effects:

- Death
- Drowsiness at bedtime, resulting in sleep
- Double vision
- Triple vision
- Inability to stop at just one Lay's Potato Chip

Avoid using Placebo-tine while driving, operating heavy machinery, or diapering an infant. Do not share Placebo-tine with any of your hypochondriac friends. Do not take Placebo-tine on an empty stomach, full stomach, or partially full stomach.

Do not take Placebo-tine if:

- you are dead
- your doctor has warned you not to die
- your doctor recommends that you should not take Placebo-tine (duh!)
- your doctor is double-billing Medicare

Before taking Placebo-tine, ask your healthcare provider:

- whether your imaginary ailment is fatal
- how to use a defibrillator on yourself
- his/her advice about that terrifying medical hoax you found online
- how to get a second, third and fourth opinion

Discontinue Placebo-tine immediately and call your healthcare provider if you experience any of the following:

- Death
- Hiccups that last more than 4 weeks
- Irresistible urge to go line dancing
- Hallucinating that you are a housefly walking on the ceiling

THOSE FABULOUS ROYALS

Why does Queen Elizabeth carry a purse everywhere she goes?

Because Prince Philip refuses to carry it for her.

What's in that purse, anyway?

Chapstick, pepper spray, lottery tickets, photo ID, hand sanitizer, business cards, earbuds, list of computer passwords, and a Swiss army knife.

What purpose does the monarchy serve in the modern world?

Through good times and bad, the royal family unites all citizens of the United Kingdom in the common complaint that the royals suck up obscene amounts of taxpayer money.

And just as the U.S. government buys soybeans and livestock to subsidize farmers, the royal family subsidizes names to keep them in circulation. For instance, King Edward VIII, who abdicated the throne in 1936, was christened Edward George Andrew Michael Romey Harold Vera Chuck and Dave.

Speaking of King Edward: he stepped down from the throne to marry American divorcee Wallis Simpson. Was he a scoundrel who shirked his duty at a crucial time in England's history?... or a sophisticated man of the world whose nuanced approach to marriage was rejected by his narrow-minded family?

Yes.

You mentioned "obscene amounts of taxpayer money." Why are the royals so expensive?

They own many lavish households, including Buckingham Palace in London, Balmoral Castle in Scotland, a lake cottage up north in Hayward, Wisconsin, and a condo in Playa del Carmen, Mexico, which is pretty much of a dump but they keep it anyway for sentimental reasons.

Each residence requires specialized staff. In Balmoral there's the Washer of the Wellies, who hoses down the queen's boots after she goes mucking about on muddy pathways. Buckingham Palace's Royal Roller keeps all 642 bathrooms supplied with Windsor-crested toilet paper. Someone has to keep track of their priceless china and silverware, then order more after a state dinner, because invariably some pieces get "borrowed" by ambassadors from certain nations we won't mention.

Members of the royal family also maintain extensive wardrobes. It wouldn't do for the queen to be seen in a bright blue chemise in Warsaw on Tuesday and the same chemise in Johannesburg on Wednesday. Even when closer to home, she changes clothes several times daily: a tapa-cloth wrap for breakfast with the delegation from Papua New Guinea, a fluffy frock for touring a denture-manufacturing facility in the posh part of Birmingham, and a glittering gown for a gala honoring The Poor Old Sods Who Lost Their Family Inheritance When We Got Kicked Out of India. Once a dress is worn in public, the queen must never wear it again — so local women queue up at charity shops every Thursday hoping for the bargain of a lifetime when the queen's discarded dresses get dropped off.

As for the Windsor men, the Royal Medal-Maker constantly invents new categories to keep them from feeling useless. Each requires expensive precious metals and stones. Prince Philip's medal for the Royal Order of the Garter Snake has green emerald eyes and a 14-karat-gold tongue. Prince Charles has nine medals, including one commissioned by the queen "on the occasion of hanging in there 53 years waiting for me to die so you could ascend to the throne."

You might have noticed that the queen has a thing about hats. Some are inspired by Dr. Suess's "The Cat in the Hat," others by the Mad Hatter of "Alice in Wonderland," and still others by Kentucky Derby hats seen on socialites who've had too many mint juleps. The queen's hats are festooned with ribbons, feathers, pompoms, flowers made of folded Kleenex, scraps of vintage wallpaper, random pieces from old games of Clue, Stone Age arrowheads, marbles, and Silly Putty. None of these come cheap. The Royal Milliner sources her material from all over the world, and the moment a seller realizes that the Windsors are involved, the asking price (even for marbles) rises exponentially.

NOSTALGIA AIN'T WHAT IT USED TO BE

While my kids sit in the dentist's chair getting their teeth cleaned, they can watch a movie, play with helium balloons, and pet a miniature pony. I tell them visiting the dentist in the '60s was a nightmare, but they don't believe me. Can you provide details?

Yes indeedy. In those days, sugar was one of the basic four food groups. Your parents only took you to the dentist every few years, and by then you had a dozen cavities the size of moon craters.

Let the anxiety begin! Mom opens the door to the dental office and shoves you inside, where a wave of *Eau de Disinfectant* slaps your nostrils. The waiting room has no toys or games, just dog-eared copies of "Woman's Day" and "Life." You squirm on a rigid plastic chair, trying to ignore the clamor of drills and jackhammers in the treatment room. Mom tells you to stop swinging your feet against the chair legs. The shrill screams of a patient rise above the power-tool racket. Mom tells you to stop sucking your thumb.

Before you can hatch an emergency escape plan, it's your turn. Mom pulls you into the torture chamber. A hefty nurse straps you into the dental chair with arm restraints and ankle cuffs. The nurse never smiles. She has warts and a prominent mustache. Is this the last thing you'll see before you die?

Enter Dr. Cadaverino. He pokes around your mouth with a sharp object and a mirror, *tsk-tsk*ing as he goes. The nurse inserts a suction tube in your mouth and randomly squirts your teeth with water. She and the doctor never speak; they've been doing this routine together since the days of the Third Reich.

Dr. Cadav wields a Novocain needle the size of a turkey baster. He picks the most exquisitely sensitive spot in your mouth for the injection site. You nearly black out from the pain. You wish you'd gone to confession last weekend.

Within a few minutes, your entire head is so numb that it rolls to one side at a 90-degree angle. Nurse Mustache places bolster panels beside each ear to keep your head straight. As Dr. Cadav drills, grinds, and hammers, Nurse M leaves the room. The suction tube slides out from beneath your tongue and starts sucking your chin. Drool runs from your mouth, flooding the flimsy paper napkin draped around your neck. Dr. Cadav doesn't notice. He's putting all his weight behind the sledgehammer. You're vaguely aware that having a railroad spike driven into your molars will have ramifications once the Novocain wears off.

After eons pass, and every surface of every tooth has been blasted, pounded and power-sanded, Dr. Cadaverino reluctantly concludes that there's nothing more he can do to you. He disappears. Nurse Mustache lifts you out of the chair and drags you back to the waiting room.

Mom writes a check for the butcher's bill, muttering that your disgraceful teeth will drive your family to the poorhouse. As a parting gesture, the desk clerk gives you a raspberry sucker. You know candy is what drove you to the torture chair. You realize you're being played for a fool to ensure repeat business. But you haven't had sugar for at least 90 minutes, and you really, *really* deserve a consolation prize, so you pop that sucker into your mouth. Mmmmmm.

My parents said we're lucky to be living in a "smart" house. Doesn't everybody?

No. Once upon a time, everybody's house was dumb. Some were dumber than others. Some were exceedingly dumb. Here's a breakdown.

A merely dumb house didn't have voice-activated electronic systems that could prepare supper, make travel arrangements, or lock/unlock doors. Rather, all those tasks were assigned to a carbon-based life-form: Mom.

"Mom, I lost my key at school. Open the door and lemme in!"

"Mom, my Cub Scout troop is coming over for supper in five minutes. Can you make Sloppy Joes?"

"Honey, I left my airline tickets in the trousers you just washed. Call the travel agent and ask them to print a new set, OK?"

A dumber house didn't have security features. If you wanted to know who just rang the doorbell, you had to peep through an eyehole, then decide whether to listen to a pitch for Fuller Brushes, Girl Scout cookies, or eternal salvation. If your house was burglarized, the only surveillance evidence was the 10-foot hole dynamited through the family room wall.

This dumber house also didn't water the lawn, cut the grass, or fix household appliances. These functions belonged to another carbon-based lifeform: Dad.

An exceedingly dumb house didn't use sensors to warn of major malfunctions. If the basement flooded, you noticed a lake rising up the basement stairs. If the furnace conked out overnight, there were icicles on your toothbrush.

Home entertainment options were bleak. The black-and-white TV in your living room got its signal through an antenna on your roof. You couldn't talk to the TV. It was really dumb. You walked over to it, pressed a button to turn it on, and turned a dial to review all three — yes, three — networks. If you liked a program, you'd better be ready to watch it in real time, or wait forever for something called "reruns."

And yet, **a modern smart house does many dumb things** that no old-fashioned dumb, dumber or exceedingly dumb house would ever do. A modern smart house…

- broadcasts your family's intimate conversations to unsuspecting strangers
- sends 156 text alerts as a squirrel jumps around on your lawn
- starts making espresso at 3 a.m.
- opens the blinds while you're walking around the bedroom in your underwear
- limits you to three-minute showers to conserve water
- doles out only four toilet flushes per day
- instructs your toddler to climb out of her crib and beg for Gummi Bears
- triggers a civil war among incompatible devices
- lectures you about your weird taste in movies

Mom and Dad said banks used to give out free toasters when they opened a savings account. They're kidding, right?

Not at all, you little whippersnapper. Here's a partial list of bank freebies: toaster, ashtray, bunk bed, Chevrolet station wagon, washer/dryer combo, belt-massager (a primitive weight-loss system), 1,380-square-foot ranch house, and ranch house lawn (sod installation included).

On the other hand, the only way to access your money was to get in that Chevrolet station wagon, drive to the bank building, wait in line, and ask the teller for $10 cash to tide you over for a week. Not very efficient, but it did cut down on impulse purchases.

HOBBY FARMING: DON'T GROW THERE

What's the difference between a hobby farm and a working farm?

Hobby farmers don't expect their farm to provide income. Working farmers expect to be millions of dollars in debt.

Would I make a good hobby farmer?

Hobby farming is in your future if:

- You enjoy the idea of farming but have never even driven past a farm.
- Most of your knowledge of farming come from watching syndicated reruns of "Green Acres."
- You've already chosen names for dozens of your future chickens.
- You subscribe to several hobby-farm magazines with centerfolds of expensive tractors.
- You assume that feeding farm animals is as simple as buying bags of Purina Horse Chow, Chicken Chow, Pig Chow, Sheep Chow and Cow Chow.

How hard can it be to become a hobby farmer, anyway?

Buying a farm? Easy. Running it? Not so much.

But running the farm would be fantastic! I'd wake up to the crowing of our rooster, have a hearty breakfast of eggs and bacon sourced at our farm, go driving around the pasture for a couple of hours on my shiny new tractor, hang out with the sheep for a bit, ride one of our horses, and finish up by petting our friendly goats.

Yeah, sure. Here's how your typical day hits the fan:

Your rooster begins crowing at 3 a.m., and by 5 a.m. you give up trying to sleep. Your hens aren't laying eggs for some gol-darn reason, so you eat Frosted Mini-Wheats for breakfast. Likewise, your visions of dining on pork from your farm, randomly driving around the pasture, riding horses, and petting friendly goats — they're all a pipe dream.

Speaking of pipes, brush up on your pipefitting, electrical, plumbing, fence-building, and engine repair skills. Hmmm, wait a minute. You never had any of these skills. So budget an extra $2 million for professionals to do the job right. Under no circumstances should you attempt half-arsed repairs on your own.

I'm tired of holding down a dull job just to bring home the bacon. I'd rather control the process from start to finish.

Hoo-boy, right, let's talk bacon. You might have a hazy understanding that bacon comes from pigs. Which means you think you want to be a pig farmer. *Do you have any idea how much pigs STINK?* The smell of pig manure from Midwestern farms can be detected at McMurdo Research Station in Antarctica.

You will need to maintain a manure pit, in which nitrogen from pig manure converts to ammonia. Peee-yewwww! This odor clings to everything you own — trucks, household furnishings, children. Most disgustingly, it clings to you. Even the other farmers you encounter at the farm co-op will backpedal as you walk by.

To lessen the stink, you'd need to give your pigs special food that reduces the amount of manure solids they excrete and improves the viscosity of their manure so it's less likely to stick to the sides of the pit, and — yucckk, ptoooeeyy! We don't even want to think about it.

Abandon your foolish quest. Leave the pig farming to working farmers, and buy your bacon at Publix.

All right, then, no pigs. How about sheep?

You probably don't know anything about sheep, either. Maybe you expect your sheep to speak perfect English like in the movie "Babe." But real sheep just *baa baa baa* all day long. It's beyond monotonous.

Sheep pack together tightly, like a clique of teenage girls, because they're prey animals. They need constant reassurance that there aren't any scary things nearby, like wolves, dogs, fence posts, trees, butterflies, or dandelion fluff. No wonder a vast herd of sheep can be intimidated and rounded up by a single border collie. Can you imagine a herd of bison acting like that? An alpha male bison would charge that dog and flip it in the air like a pancake.

So forget about wandering around with your flock. If you get closer than a half-mile, the sheep will take off running to the other end of the pasture. You *did* put up fencing, right? If not, they'll run to the nearest freeway, try to cross it, create an immense backup of traffic — and your goofy farm will be the top story on the nightly news.

One exception to timid sheep is a dominant male ram, the self-appointed Leader of the Pack. Never turn your back on him, or you'll appreciate where the term "ram" comes from.

We've got to have horses!

Oh, really? You should know that seasoned owners call horses "eggs on legs." They're the NFL quarterbacks of your farm, capable of moments of brilliant athleticism followed by long periods on the injured reserve. What's more, they produce about 50 pounds of manure, *per horse,* per day.

Organic farmers say you can compost this waste for use in garden-ing, although they admit that composting "takes some effort." (Yeah, just like building the ancient Egyptian pyramids of Giza "took some bricks.") You need to build a compost bin, scrape up horse manure from the pasture and dump it in the bin, water the manure, layer it with leaves, turn the pile to add oxygen, and so on. Or, forget composting. Just keep dumping raw manure in a corner of the pasture until it's high enough to make a ski hill in the winter.

When visiting a breeder, demonstrate your shrewd horse-trading skills with these questions.

- How much are you asking for this horse? (Pick yourself up from the barn floor.) Seriously? (Catch your breath.) Do you take American Express?
- Is this a boy horse or a girl horse?
- What are those iron things on the bottom of its feet? Do they come in different colors?
- Has the horse had any professional training? Acting lessons? Dancing lessons?
- Does this horse have any bad habits like biting people, stepping on people, or kidnapping people?
- Has the horse ever had hip replacement surgery or a facelift?
- Why are you laughing at me?

We're thinking of raising chickens, too.

OK. First, identify your goals. Are you raising chickens for eggs, for meat, or just to scratch around and ruin your flowerbeds?

Fun fact #1: Eggs containing baby chicks can be safely mailed to you. They're even eligible for Amazon Prime. Hatcheries guarantee the breed and sex of the hatchlings. Your children can learn valuable life lessons watching the chicks peck out of their shells. If some of the female chicks you ordered turn out to be roosters, the kids will learn deeper lessons about coping with adversity. Do you attempt to send the little roosters back? Surreptitiously drop them in the hatchling bin at the Rural King store? Help the kids build a lemonade stand for a special sale of "buy one lemonade, get one chick free"?

Fun fact #2: The old phrase "running around like a chicken with its head cut off" isn't an exaggeration. That poultry-zombie makes a gruesome sight. Don't bring out the guillotine until your kids have left for school in the morning.

If your chickens are destined for future batches of chicken soup, do not give them names. Taking a hatchet to an unnamed chicken is hard enough; decapitating little Henny Penny is impossible.

Raising chickens for their eggs adds a whole new level of complexity. At times, the "girls" simply stop laying. In that case you must add more protein to their diet, in the form of pumpkin seeds, mealworms, Clif Builder's Energy Bars, or Power Crunch Wafer Crème Protein Bars. Eggs themselves are another good source of protein, but that raises the ugly specter of chicken cannibalism. Besides, where will the eggs come from if your hens aren't laying? It's the old story: which came first, the non-laying chicken or the nonexistent egg? Forget that we mentioned it.

Chickens love routine, and the slightest change in schedule can upset their laying habits. Have you changed their tea time, the at-home-visiting hours from neighboring hens, or the HBO series they're allowed to watch?

Certain breeds don't lay as many eggs, or don't lay eggs at all. This may be the case if you bought a "fancy" chicken because she matches your family room drapes. That's like marrying a supermodel and becoming upset when she doesn't want kids.

And here's a final word about roosters. You should keep a rooster only if (1) your entire family is deaf, and (2) you hate everyone who lives within 10 miles of your farm.

Cows grazing in the pasture look so peaceful. I see a herd of dairy cows in our future.

Dairy farming is a life sentence of hard labor. See those big protrusions beneath the females? Those are known as "udders." They need to be emptied of milk at least twice a day, every day, forever and ever. It's your job to draw out that milk into metal pails, a large-capacity milking machine, or cute mason jars (1,000 per day) to sell at a weekly farmer's market.

On the brighter side, economists tell us that one dairy cow creates four full-time jobs in the local community. She might handle payroll and human relations at a local factory, for example. Cows make excellent sous chefs and sommeliers. They're also skilled at coding — a talent in high demand at software firms.

So, between milking chores and chauffeuring your cows to their day jobs, you'll be running ragged. But even that's not the end of it. Consider that a dairy cow produces 125 pounds of saliva per day. Who's going to mop up all that spit? Y-O-U, that's who.

The cow salivates so much because she drinks at least 50 gallons of water each day. That's more than enough to fill a Jacuzzi. One of the few complaints office managers have about cow employees is the excessive amount of time they hang around the water cooler.

In terms of daily feed, your cows need both roughage and protein. Principal sources of roughage are pastureland, hay, and Wheaties. Protein comes from alfalfa hay and protein supplements available in any health food store. Don't try giving them Muscle Milk, though. The name freaks them out.

We'll also get some goats. Our kids loved them at the petting zoo.

Fifteen minutes at the petting zoo proves nothing; your children will lose interest in all your farm animals within two minutes. Yet there are other reasons for keeping goats. They have really weird eyes that can hypnotize people into doing their will. No wonder your hard-core survivalist neighbors believe goats are the spawn of Satan. If you keep goats, those neighbors will leave you alone.

Goats are highly intelligent, although you might not guess it as they munch on tin cans, wire, your shirttail, and the roof of the nice shelter you bought for them. Once they're done dining on shingles, they jump off the roof, clear the pasture fence and head out to scare the horses. Goats have also been known to climb to the tops of cars, trucks, barns, gas stations and public libraries. Some animal behaviorists believe this is a sign of condescension: the goats want to look down on everybody else. Or maybe they're just nuts.

I want a bright, shiny new tractor!

This is definitely a guy thing. Owning a hobby farm is just your excuse to buy a tractor, anticipating the carefree fun of simply driving around the property. But listen up: your hobby farm actually does require a tractor — for hard chores you've never imagined:

Bush hogging

No, this doesn't involve pushing around stinky pigs — "bush hogging" means mowing heavy brush. This is especially fun in steamy midsummer heat with nasty flies bouncing off your head and dive-bombing your eyes. Too bad you can't swish them away with a tail like your cows and horses do.

Emergency transport

A tractor enables you to tend livestock during a blizzard, flood or other natural disaster. It also helps you get to town after you've lost your driver's license for a DUI violation.

Building fences

The grass is always greener at your neighbor's farm, because he knows 100% more about proper fertilizer and irrigation than you do. Livestock prefer green fields; therefore, you must fence them in. The tractor can carry 80-pound rolls of barbed wire, post hole digger, fence stretcher and steel posts, so you can drop them way out in the field and leave them there while you Google "fence-building."

Backhoeing

A backhoe attached to your tractor can carry at least a week's worth of horse doodoo. Be sure to overload the bucket and lift it high so the entire tractor tips over and buries you in manure. Ask someone to record this on video; you might go viral on TikTok or YouTube.

THE GUYS' CRAP ROADSHOW

Hello, everyone, and welcome to the latest edition of The Guys' Crap Roadshow on PBS. Tonight we're broadcasting from beautiful Decatur, Illinois. As always, we've selected several local guys out of the hundreds who brought their crap to be appraised. Will it be trash, or treasure? Let's find out!

Our first submission belongs to Mr. Gary Indiana. Is that right? Your name is Gary Indiana, but you live in Illinois?

Yup. There's too many Garys in Indiana. But here, I can stand out a little.

OK. Now tell us about your piece of crap.

Yeah, well, this here's my recliner. My wife threatened to leave it at the curb for the garbage collector. I want to keep using it in the living room. We went halfway: if it's worth more than $20, I get to keep it, but at less than $20, it's history.

All right, let's have a look. Well, well, there's lots of wear on the headrest and armrests.

That's because this is genuine pleather.

Artificial leather, yes.

They don't make 'em like that anymore.

Not since the pleather recall of 1986. Would you please sit in the chair and demonstrate the reclining mechanism?

Sure thing. <chunkkk!> <sproing!> <donnggg!>

Quite heavy switching through the gears.
I got it finessed just the way I like it.

What's this wooden handle beneath the footrest? Is that a…hammer?
Uh, yeah. Once in a while the gears need recalibrating. Well, what d'ya think? Don't you need to check the blue book value?

That won't be necessary. I'm sorry to say that I'm valuing your chair at 50 cents.
Aw, dang!

Shall we send it to the recycling area? That way you won't need to transport it back home.
I guess so. Just let me sit in it awhile and say goodbye.

Take all the time you need. We're moving on to our second guy. Your name, sir?
Joe Strzykanjynczkinski.

Thanks. I was having trouble reading your nametag.
It doesn't have enough room for all my syllables.

And the object you've brought is — what, exactly?
It's a beard.

A…beard?
One hundred percent human hair, yes, sir.

It seems to be holding up remarkably well, considering that it's not on a face.
Back in the old country, they knew how to remove a beard in one piece with kerosene, and preserve the shape by dipping it in varnish.

And how did you come by this beard, Joe?

It's been in our family for five generations. My great-great-great *pradziadek* grew it originally. Then each family handed it down to their eldest son. Every Christmas we do the *dekoracja* — that's when we hang the beard on the tip of an upside-down blue spruce and sing "Jolly Jolly Christmas Tree."

I can just imagine.

We always have a couple dozen toasts with *krupnik,* too. Everybody gets a turn, even the kids.

The kids drink this "krupnik"?

Oh, yeah. It's great to be Polish! You should try it sometime.

Well, Joe, I must say this is a first. I have no idea what the market value of this beard would be. But considering its sentimental value, I suggest you keep it in the family.

Yeah, I was gonna do that anyway. I just hoped you'd quote a high number so I'd have something to say to the guys at the plant where I work. They're always giving me grief about this beard. But is this any weirder than a Christmas fruitcake that keeps going back and forth for 50 years?

Yes, it's much weirder than a fruitcake.

OK, I guess so.

Let's move on to our next guy — Jake Symons. Jake, what have you brought for us today?

I've got a world-class inventory of hardware. Little hardware, I mean. Fasteners and nails and screws and hooks, whatever you need.

Each of these 5-gallon pails is full of fasteners?

Yup, every single one.

Let's see…this pail has screws…wait, there's also some nails and… other things…

Yeah, I haven't gotten around to sorting them yet.

"Yet"? Are these new?

No, I got them from my uncle about 20, 30 years ago.

There's lots of rust on these pieces.

Yeah. But they still work fine.

Seven pails full.

Hey, you can always use a nail or a picture hanger or something. You know what they say: "Better to have and not need than to need and not have."

We often hear that from our guests.

So, how about it? Pretty valuable, huh?

Let's see. Those pails must weigh at least 60 pounds each. Seven pails. Multiply seven times $25 — that's $175.

Wow, $175, that's great! I'm gonna put that toward a tree saddle hunting platform for deer season.

No, Jake, you don't understand. We're going to *charge* you $175 for taking these pails to a recycling center — unless you want to reclaim them?

Well, yeah, of course. I'll still use them someday. "Better to have —"

OK, Jake. Well, folks, that's all we have time for today. Thanks for watching, everybody! Check our website to see when The Guys' Crap Roadshow is coming to your town!

WHEN SPIES NEED A SHRINK

From the archives of Alexander Waverly,
Spy Shrink, MD, PhD, LLC, U.N.C.L.E.

Mrs. James Bond Begins Couples Therapy — Alone

Good afternoon, madam. I'm Dr. Waverly.

Hello, doctor. I'm Mrs. Bond. Mrs. James Bond.

And you're interested in couples therapy. Is that right?

That's correct. My husband, Mr. Bond — James Bond — agreed to come with me today, but he was called away at the last minute.

We can work around that. Perhaps your husband might join us next time.

I'm sure he would like to, just as he agreed earlier, but something came up. That's the problem. Something always comes up. Like today — we were halfway out the door when the panic button on his wristband started flashing. He said he was urgently needed in Istanbul, called a cab for me, and ran up 110 flights of stairs to the helipad on the roof of our high-rise.

Does your husband frequently travel for work?

He travels constantly. Yet I have no idea what he does, or for whom.

He never shares this information with you?

Once, just once, he slipped up and told me his boss is called "M," but he made me promise to keep it to myself. He said I'd be in danger if I knew anything more. Can you imagine? I'm his wife, Mrs. Bond, Mrs. James Bond, and I'm not supposed to know why he keeps a folding knife in the waistband of his briefs? Or why sultry women arrive at our condo asking to see him? When I answer the door, they mistake me for his housekeeper, for heaven's sake! I inform them I'm Mrs. Bond, Mrs. James Bond, and they seem surprised that there *is* a Mrs. James Bond.

Do you ever suspect him of…indiscretions?

I don't just suspect it, I'm sure of it. On the rare occasions when he does come home, there's a different color of lipstick on his collar, every single time. He changes shirts in the lobby.

Excuse me, I'm confused. If he changes shirts in the lobby, how do you —

I bribed the concierge. We kept getting outrageous bills from the dry cleaners. I had to know why.

I see. So, Mrs. Bond —

Mrs. James Bond.

Yes, Mrs. James Bond, it seems you're at an impasse. Your entire self-image is bound up in a man who's physically and emotionally unavailable. What would you hope to accomplish in couples therapy?

Well, you're right about my self-image. I do want to remain Mrs. James Bond.

But do you think your husband will change?

I don't expect him to give up those sultry women. I just want a date night every couple of years. Maybe a bouquet of flowers now and then — but not flowers regifted from the penthouse at the Mandarin Oriental in Singapore. A full night together in the same bed. That sort of thing.

Those are modest goals, to be sure. I think there's a good chance he might agree, once you tell him how much this means to you.

And when you lead the discussion, that would really help.

Would you like to set up another appointment?

Yes, I would. Before he left for Istanbul, I asked my husband — Mr. Bond, Mr. James Bond — about his availability for a new session.

What would be most convenient for both of you?

Do you have any openings in, say, the year 2035?

Jason Bourne Hasn't Slept in a Month

Welcome, Mr. Bourne. Have a seat anywhere you like.

Um, I'd rather stand.

Please, Mr. Bourne. We need to sit down and maintain eye contact while we talk.

Well, OK, but I'm turning this chair so I won't have my back to the door.

Yes, just sit comfortably and try to relax.

This room has four chairs, a couch, one exit, and a statue of the Buddha in a little water fountain. Why do I notice these things? What's wrong with me?

I suppose you're just…observant. Now, what's the main concern that brings you here?

I don't really know who I am.

Yes, I see. The existential crisis. That's typical among my patients.

No, it's not a philosophical thing. I actually don't know who I am, period. I think of myself as Jason Bourne, but there are 16 passports in the junk drawer of my kitchen, all with my picture but different names: John Smith, Yuri Slivovitz, Sean O'Clock. Some mornings I wake up with injuries I don't remember getting, like big bruises. Ugly gashes. Tattoos, even.

That's a real beauty on your arm. A Mexican cutie, is it?

Yeah, but I don't have a clue how it got there. Listen, doc, could you at least give me some extra-strength sleeping pills?

Medication is only indicated in severe cases. Self-calming routines and social support work best for most people. Do you have friends or relatives you can talk to when you're especially anxious?

Well, there is this woman from work, but I think she's getting sick of hearing me say the same thing, time after time.

What's that?

I say, "Get some rest, Pam. You look tired."

Illya Kuryakin, That Other Man from U.N.C.L.E.

Illya, my friend! It's been so long. How are you?

Not very well, Mr. Waverly.

That's *Doctor* Waverly.

Oh yes. Dr. Waverly.

How can I help you?

I've been having flashbacks. Feeling left out. Resentful. Filled with despair.

Wonderful!

Excuse me?

Err, I mean it's wonderful that you've come for therapy. Now tell me, how long have you been feeling this way?

Ever since I joined U.N.C.L.E and teamed up with Napoleon Solo.

Ah, the amazing Mr. Solo! Our brilliant Agent Number One. They've retired his number, you know. And now he's got an outstanding career with the CIA.

I know. People still go on and on about him.

Yes, Solo's very talented. Widely respected.

On and on.

One of the CIA's best operatives, actually.

And on and on.

He's the head of CIA's division to counter our old archenemy, Thrush. I can't say enough about him.

Helloooo. That's why I came to see you. Everybody focuses on Solo. They always did. He got the girls and the glory. I was second best.

But that's not true. You were always third best.

What?!

I was second best. And come to think of it, that "tailor" in the fake storefront entrance to our headquarters had such presence. Best faux tailor I've ever worked with. So he's third best in our agency rankings. That would make you fourth best.

I knew it! I was nothing but comic relief!

But Illya, you were jolly good at comic relief. Like in The Slapstick Affair, when the bad guys left a banana peel on the sidewalk, and you slipped and fell on your bum.

I didn't join the agency to become a clown!

Then you and Solo did The Whoopee Cushion Affair. Oh my word, those noises whenever you sat down — blaaaap blaaaap blaaaap! Hilarious!

I don't believe this.

And how about The Oscar Mayer Wiener Affair, when you — I say, Illya, where are you going?

I've had it, *Doctor* Waverly. I'm going to join Thrush!

CARSON'S SECOND ELEVEN: THESE ARE PRETTY GOOD, TOO

INFERIOR DECORATING

Beautify Your Baffroom

By guest columnist Angie Airhead

Our guest bathroom needs updating. How can we freshen the look and make our guests feel welcome?

Great question! Some homeowners feel it's enough to set out a roll of toilet paper and a bar of soap. But I say, take it up a notch and create bathroom magic!

Most decorators would tell you to choose artwork or new light fixtures first. They're wrong, dead wrong. Go for the **shower curtain** first. It sets the tone for the whole room, whether it's flowered or striped, or…um…blue or red or green or whatever, and made of cloth or plastic, recycled soda bottles, or woven llama hair. You could go bonkers in Bed Bath & Beyond looking at all the choices. In fact, I got lost in there just the other day and ended up buying a stand mixer instead.

Next, choose an **area rug** for the area in front of the sink, or the area in front of the toilet, or the area next to the shower. The main thing is that it should sit on an area. Otherwise, it's not an area rug. You could also buy area rugs for all three areas. If your guest bathroom is small, these three area rugs might overlap. In the decorating trade, this is known as a carpet.

Now that you've got the shower curtain and area rugs, buy some **towels.** Nowadays, people expect towels in the guest bath. If you forget to set out towels, they can get quite grumpy. Nobody likes to dry their hands on flimsy toilet paper or the front of their jeans. So get towels in colors that sort of go with the rest of the décor. Sometimes you can find monogrammed towels online for bargain prices, especially if they're embroidered with unpopular initials like Z or Q.

Selecting a **paint** color is next. Did you know that walls reflect light onto your guests when they look in the mirror? You don't want pukey-green faces staring back at them; they might blame your cooking. To test a color scheme, buy white poster boards and several samples of paint. Paint each poster board with one color, then hold the board behind your head while looking in the mirror. Do you look flushed, like you've had too much booze? Or greenish from food poisoning? Or blue, with dark circles under your eyes from trying to sleep on a too-soft mattress? If you're still not sure, cover your face with paint and look again.

Next up is the **artwork.** By now you've got plenty of color going on: towels, shower curtain, area rugs, and paint. Which colors are missing? Maybe you don't have any Pepto-Bismol pink, or slime green, or earthworm brown. Look up an online art store and click the color selector tool. You'll see page after page of art in your special color.

Choose a really unusual picture — like maybe a pygmy hippo, or a nude couple running on the beach, or a bunch of melting watches by that artist Salvador Dolly. Get this picture printed in the largest size you can afford. Put it in a gilded frame or something classy like that. Then hang it over the toilet, so your guests won't notice that you haven't scrubbed the toilet. If you're worried that they'll notice anyway, set out one of those plastic toilet brushes with its own holder. Maybe include a pair of rubber gloves if your guests are persnickety. Oh — sorry, I forgot — also make sure the picture is framed under glass, because when it's hanging over the toilet, anything can happen.

Now for a really fun decorating idea: **baskets!** You can go crazy with this! Some of my radical ideas for filling baskets: rolled-up towels and washcloths, candles, scented soap, potpourri, and crinkly raffia paper. Bet you've never seen these accessories before! To make the basket really swanky, add one of those air freshener sprays or ceramic soap dishes you swiped while visiting a friend's house.

Now, take the final step to make the room guest-ready: rearrange the medicine cabinet. Clear out your stash of prescription painkillers, medical marijuana and what-have-you, and hide it in a hiding place where no one ever goes. Replace this stuff with practical-joke toys like chattering teeth or a rubber chicken that will fall forward when the door opens. If your guests freak out, well, serves them right for snooping.

Midcentury Modern Madness

By guest columnist Vera Cynical

What is midcentury modern design?

The original midcentury modernists in the 1950s created a futuristic look. Designers borrowed heavily from significant trendsetters like *The Jetsons*.

Today, you'll see midcentury furnishings and exteriors in which basic elements of design are uglified.

...for example?

Dressers with toothpick legs. Coffee tables shaped like kidney beans. Dining room sets made of natural elements like porcupine hide, oriented strand board, and twisted iron. Exteriors in which brick walls are interrupted by random panels of stark metal, as if the builder ran out of bricks.

Which colors are associated with midcentury modern style?

Pumpkin orange, avocado green, and mustard yellow work well with this design. As a bonus, they'll perk up your appetite.

Didn't we all just replace our avocado-green refrigerators, pumpkin-orange shag carpeting, and mustard-yellow side chairs?

Please don't bring that up.

I'd like to start small — maybe with a couple of midcentury lighting fixtures.

You could try a Sputnik chandelier and a tripod floor lamp. These are popular "statement" pieces that announce: "I'm aiming for a retro look but afraid to go all-in on fad furniture."

What other elements are popular?

A metal and glass bar cart turns an ordinary living room into a spectacular place to get roaring drunk. Stocked with a generous supply of liquor, the cart enables you and your guests to ignore the ugliness of your other mod furnishings. At the end of the night, you can wheel it out to the driveway as a subtle signal that everyone should go home.

Stiff plastic dust covers on the sofa, armchairs and lampshades create that sought-after "don't touch" look.

Aluminum Christmas trees are back in style. And considering how much they cost, you might want to keep this bristling tannenbaum on display all year long.

Last but not least: installing *a huge sunburst mirror* above the family-room sofa will establish that you're on-trend, special, and unique — just like everyone else.

Home Staging: Lipstick on a Pig

By guest columnist Theresa "Tough Love" Jones,
National Organization of Staging Experts (NOSE)

After 28 years in the same house, we're finally putting it on the market. We've heard that "staging" will make it sell faster and bring a higher price. What do we need to know?

Are you serious — 28 years?! Why not just take a flame-thrower and…okay, hold on. <deep breath, deep breath> Yes, I have some advice for you.

This is no time for mere winnowing or Kondo-ing. Hire a professional stager to throw all your junk into a Dumpster so the interior no longer resembles a landfill.

Professional stagers will also…

…bring in new living room and dining furniture that isn't stained, worn, or covered with pet hair.

…place "occasional" chairs that occasionally disappear and reappear without notice.

…create a realistic, homey look with a fake laptop computer, bowls of plastic fruit, and inflatable beds.

For all of this expertise, home staging is a bargain at $1,000 to $5,000 or more, depending on how much the home stager guesses you'll fork over.

A thousand bucks?! How about some stage-it-yourself ideas?

Okay, cheapskate. Here are a few basics:

Help prospective buyers imagine themselves living in your home. Place a bag of tortilla chips and a half-empty jar of cheese dip on the coffee table. Scatter big tumbleweeds of dog hair on hard-surface floors. Leave the toilets unflushed.

Redecorate. You should look as if you're an Ikea and Crate & Barrel family instead of a Walmart and Scavenging Roadside Furniture Left Out For The Garbage Truck family. That means "yes" to tasteful abstract prints on the wall, "no" to NASCAR posters… "yes" to a beige cashmere throw casually draped across the sofa, "no" to a flannel SpongeBob SquarePants sleeping bag…"yes" to table settings of pure white china, "no" to chipped maroon melamine.

Use color, furniture placement, and flashing neon lights to draw attention to your home's best features.

Our house has doesn't have any good features.

Gosh, what a surprise. Then you'll have to invent some. One look that's really trending right now is to place white covers on all the books in your library.

We don't have books. The only thing we ever read is the numbers on our scratch-off lottery tickets.

So you're one of *those* families. You probably watch lots of TV.

Oh, yeah! We've got a huge flat-screen, and it's turned on all the time.

Ugh. Interior designers loathe TVs. In fact, licensed designers take a blood oath to hide every single TV in a client's home. We recommend covering your TV with a large placemat. Or install drywall over it. If you absolutely must keep it turned on during an open house, run upbeat family movies like "Scarface" and "Casino."

Our real estate broker told us we should bake chocolate chip cookies right before an open house.

Ah, the old chocolate chip cookie ploy. I've got news for you: cookies won't last more than five minutes. Your family will glom them down on their way out the door. If you really want fragrance, burn cash. That's right, set paper money in a fireproof dish and light a match to it. Don't skimp, either. Use fifty- and hundred-dollar bills for that evocative "money pit" scent; discerning buyers will think you've spent thousands of dollars remodeling.

We don't have much time for staging. Can we do just a few rooms?

Absolutely. Potential buyers care most about the living room, master bedroom, and kitchen, so make changes there. Seal off the other rooms with yellow crime-scene tape. For your kids' messy bedrooms, nail the doors shut.

What about the outside of the house?

Curb appeal is essential, so if your street doesn't have curbs, consider renting some. Then take a hard, objective look at your front entry. Remove the fake-evergreen Christmas wreath that's been hanging on the door since 1957. That humorous "GO AWAY" doormat should go, too. Make your front door "pop" with a fresh coat of paint and some firecrackers. Inspect your lawn for spots of dead grass; spray-paint the dirt with a bright shade of green.

Once you've finished staging, just sit back, relax, and watch your house languish on the market until you drop it below a reasonable price you should have set in the first place.

Great Exhortations

Many of my friends hang cutesy signs in their houses. The signs say things like "Live, Laugh, Love" or "Make today a great day." It's stressing me out. Do I need to follow these rules even after I leave their homes?

Those aren't the Ten Commandments, sweetheart. Some people simply don't like bare walls, but they do like ordering others around.

We must all take a stand against bossy signs. Memorize these alternatives to help you keep things in perspective when someone's sign is hounding you.

For instance, instead of "You can never have too much happy," think "You can easily have too much hokey."

Welcome, please remove your shoes, thank you > Ugh, take your shoes off, you derelict

Live, Laugh, Love > Lie, Lurch, Leave

Always be humble and kind > Always be kind of hyper

This is our happy place > This is our battleground

Life is too short to drink bad wine > What kind of cheap wine did you bring?

Life isn't about waiting for the storm to pass, it's about learning to dance in the rain > Life isn't about standing outside in the rain, it's about going indoors to watch Netflix

Blessed > Stressed

The best is yet to come > The bubble is about to burst

I love you to the moon and back > I love you to the end of the driveway

Family gathers here > Pet hair gathers here

Relax > Revenge

Let your faith be bigger than your fear > Let your gut be bigger than your beer

A dream is a wish your heart makes > A poop is the squish your dog makes

Grateful > Forgetful

Make today a great day > Get this day over with

We cannot direct the wind, but we can adjust our sails > We cannot sail a boat, but we can rent a JetSki

It is what it is > What the heck is it?

CLIMATE CHANGE: DEADLY BUTTERFLIES VS. GODZILLA

Transcript of a compulsory re-education session at
The Climate Change Gulag, Berkeley, California

I don't understand the panic over climate change. What's the big deal?

It is not just a big deal, comrade. It's a catastrophe. If we don't take drastic measures, San Francisco will be underwater in a few months. All wildlife, except possibly the armadillo, will become extinct. Worst of all, everyone will lose cellphone service. And it all started with the butterfly effect.

What does the butterfly effect have to do with climate?

According to the Gospel of Climate Change (Barack 2:1–4), "Any small movement in one part of an ecosystem triggers a ripple effect. A butterfly flutters its wings, stirring the air within 5 centimeters. Then some other stuff happens. And pretty soon we're all dead."

But wouldn't the billions of butterflies in the world counteract each other? They're not fluttering their wings in unison.

One individual wouldn't have much effect if all butterflies were the same. But they're not. The newly-formed Federal Center for

Deadly-Butterfly Research* has released a shocking bulletin entitled "Deadly Butterflies Endanger All Life on Earth Except Possibly the Armadillo."

*Thank you, taxpayers, for your support.

The report says, "Butterflies emitting methane and sulfur gases will obliterate the world as we know it. Very soon. Maybe next week. It depends on how much fresh sweet corn, bell peppers and unripe bananas they eat… [etcetera, etcetera]…global adversaries [blah-blah-blah]… weaponized butterflies …noxious gas." In laymen's terms, this means foreign enemies have created deadly farting butterflies.

Oh, noooooh!

Oh yes, and the report concludes: "Considering this imminent disaster, we must immediately upgrade to DEFCON 1 status: Release Godzilla."

Godzilla, yaaay! I love Godzilla!

That's more like it, comrade. You're coming around. Just keep that nitrous oxide mask over your nose while you watch the following promotion:

"Godzilla. Who doesn't love that wacky Japanese mega-lizard who destroys tall cardboard buildings with a swipe of his jagged tail? Godzilla will square off against a roiling mass of farting butterflies this Saturday in Times Square at 8 p.m. EDT. Given the deadly effects of butterfly gas, the area will be closed to the general public, but you can catch every heart-stopping moment at home. Get exclusive real-time streaming via pay-per-view ($49.95), exclusively on ESPN-2."

I'm totally on board with this! Tell me what other climate theories I can get worked up about.

Good, very good. Memorize the following information as if your life depended on it — because it does. The Climate Change Thought

Police may visit your home at any time for mandatory testing and possible relocation to the Center for Attitude Adjustment (Electroshock Division).

Plastic drinking straws killing the ocean

Plastic straws are the third leading cause of ocean pollution, just behind excessive sunscreen (#1) and undiapered infants (#2) — and yes, how appropriate that undiapered infants are threat "number two."

Here's the official version: Somehow large groups of drinking straws discarded within the continental United States find their way into the ocean, like the cliff swallows returning to San Juan Capistrano. Yes, this includes drinking straws from deserts and landlocked states. Once in the ocean, the straws form gangs that go around bullying manatees, sea turtles, porpoises, dolphins and stingrays, and then… well, we're not quite sure what happens after that, but you can bet it's really awful.

Take the pledge to stop using plastic straws with your morning espresso. It's the least you can do, especially since you never sucked coffee through a straw anyway.

If you really need straws, get ones made of glass or metal. They come with tiny brushes that won't fit inside the straw — so when you get dysentery, just tell yourself it's all for the good of the country.

Evil methods of transportation

Planes, trains and automobiles… tour buses, dump trucks and ice cream trucks…tractors, jitneys and Formula 1 race cars…bad! All bad! Anything with a motor is bad, including your washing machine and dryer!

Did you know that if every household in the United States switched just one regular lightbulb to a CFL or LED bulb, this is equivalent to removing 1 million cars from the road? Too bad the lightbulb lobby is so entrenched in politics that this will never happen — but we *can* remove 1 million cars from the road and call it a victory in the light-bulb department.

Jet planes are really bad. Don't get us wrong — we don't mean luxury aircraft chartered by climate radicals to reach their overseas gripe-fests. After all, their time is precious. But commercial air travel that most people can afford is bad by definition, because most people can afford it.

Instead of traveling by jet to your next business conference or Disney World pilgrimage, take the train. Not just any train, but a vintage outfit like the coal-fired City of New Orleans. (We'll make allowances for coal here, because this alternative is so difficult and uncomfort-able that it's righteous.) Build an extra three months into your sched-ule to allow for mechanical breakdowns and robberies by masked bandits on horseback. Also, pack extra clothing to replace your travel garments, which will become flecked with soot and cinders. Then just sit back, relax, and deal card games with the old men in the club car.

We can also take a cue from Amish communities, which rely on horse-driven carriages. There's a downside, of course. To paraphrase what former President Obama said about electrical costs: "Under this plan, horse manure will necessarily skyrocket." We'll leave that problem for the next generation to solve. They're used to older people dumping crap all over their future.

Evil lifestyles

Cell phones…voice-driven "smart" houses…cheap plastic every-thing…taking hot baths instead of cold showers…weekly mani-cures…tossing out leftover food scraps instead of building a compost pile in the bathtub…all baaaaaaad!

Instead, we must learn to live like the Amish, with their vintage washboards, candles, hand-pumped water wells, and simple cloth-ing. It hasn't hurt them a bit. In fact, they've cornered the market* on handmade quilts and wood furniture.

The domestic market, that is. Their horses won't pull carriages into the ocean, because they know what happened to Pharaoh and his chariots and charioteers in the Red Sea.

If you'd like to test-drive (or test-buggy-ride) the Amish lifestyle, invest in plain garments and broad-rimmed headwear. Power down your cellphone and wrap it in a quilt. Churn some butter. Unplug your refrigerator.

Armadillo by morning

Armadillos are the most resilient creatures on the planet. They might even survive the upcoming climate Armageddon; after all, both armadillo and Armageddon have the prefix "arma," from the Latin "armpit." We must study and learn from them…armadillos, that is, not armpits.

Wearing a suit of corrugated armor is one good way to imitate the armadillo. This will also protect your skin without the need for evil sunscreen. Another armadillo tactic would be to strengthen your tongue, coat it with something sticky, and catch insects after digging them out of the ground. You could also scavenge for dead animals; now that you're traveling by horse-drawn carriage, you'll notice road-kill all over the place. There's even a country song by George Strait that celebrates our mascot: "Armadillo by morning / up from San Antone / bodysuit strong as iron / is all that he's got on…" What? It's actually "Amarillo by Morning"? Okay, never mind.

Locally sourced food

We admit, sometimes it's hard to know whether supermarket items have been obtained locally. How far has that head of lettuce traveled? You could ask it, but it's just a head without a mouth. Tiny stickers on Dole bananas urge you to see the latest "Lion King" movie; does that mean they were grown in Africa? Has that loaf of white balloon bread bounced around in a semi-trailer for two hours, or was it delivered by a colorful old ethnic character with a pushcart? Pester the store manager for answers to these vital questions.

Lights out

Failing to turn off lights in unused rooms is such a serious matter that Pope Francis has declared it a cardinal sin, which means that only Catholic cardinals may do so without incurring extra time in purgatory. Whenever you leave a room, even if it's just for a couple of minutes, turn off all the lights. Bonus points if your entire family is also using the room.

The bathroom

Enact a policy of flushing just once every ten uses. Post instructions above all toilets to enlighten your guests.

When it comes to personal hygiene, be aware that "The family that bathes together saves together" (saves water, that is). Once a week, draw a half-tub of tepid water for all family members to use at the same time. Trust us, any kid over age four would rather die than take a bath with Mom and Dad. Your teens will shower at the gym instead; the middle-school kids will skip showering altogether and smell much more rank than usual; and you parental units get the tub all to yourselves.

THE QUICK AND THE NOT-SO-QUICK

Is There Life After Logic?

What's up with these people claiming to visit the afterlife during a near-death experience? Are they crazy or what?

No crazier than you or me! (Well, no crazier than me, anyway. I can't vouch for you.) Read the following accounts, and decide for yourself.

Shirley B., Atlantic City, New Jersey

While lying on a gurney in the emergency room, I felt my spirit leaving my body. My spirit floated upward and bonked its head on the ceiling. A minute later, it left the ER through a ventilation duct.

I kept moving upward. The atmosphere got thinner. At about 30,000 feet, I almost collided with a Southwest Airlines 737-800. The passengers inside were immediately visible to me. They were eating tiny packets of peanuts and squirming from the lack of legroom. Farther, much farther up I flew, and the sky turned black. There were millions of stars. I'm pretty sure I saw the Big Dipper. Or maybe it was the Little Dipper. Which Dipper is the one that's upside down?

Anyway, all at once a huge castle appeared. It was made of pure light and other light things, like feathers and balsa wood. Two men stood at the entrance gate: a sentry and a bouncer. The bouncer was very muscular and intimidating, and he roared savagely, like a pro wrestler. I was afraid he would block my way, but the sentry smiled and said, "Don't mind Da Crusher. He's just here to catch any Nazis that sneak past the stratosphere." The sentry checked his clipboard and told me, "Go on in, Helen." I didn't correct him about my name. I just nodded as I floated through the gate.

In front of the castle was a big courtyard, like something you'd see at Disney World. Lots of characters in costume were dancing, along with people like me who didn't get the memo about costumes. Fake rocks stood at the edges of the courtyard; actually, they were speakers, playing songs from movie soundtracks. I bought a flashing Star Wars toy lightsaber from a roaming vendor and waved it around, just for something to do.

People were communicating telepathically with each other. We could understand one another's languages. A Japanese man told his wife they could've had this same experience at Tokyo Disneyland. A German woman asked her husband whether he'd packed his Speedo. At that point I'd had enough telepathic understanding. I asked the Higher Power to send me back to my life.

Immediately I descended through an incredibly long plastic tube, like at a water park, only without the water. It chafed my thighs something terrible. I awoke on the same gurney in the ER, just as I'd left it. The doctors marveled at my sudden recovery and wondered why my thighs were so red.

If anyone thinks they might take a journey like this, my advice is to wear a helmet and apply lots of Vaseline to their thighs.

Stan Z., South Milwaukee, Wisconsin

I was given a tour of Heaven by a shining angel with a real estate broker's license. Heaven was modeled after Detroit, which didn't exactly thrill me. Let's just say I won't be buying a condo there.

The angel gave me a guest pass and told me to wander around on my own. I didn't want to hang around, but the angel said that if I returned to my earthly body at that moment, I would be a vegetable for the rest of my life — possibly broccoli or cauliflower. I hate vegetables, so I followed the angel's instructions to kill a couple more hours in Heaven.

I found an orchard filled with fruit trees, and soup trees, cheeseburger trees and coffee trees, in that order. People were working their way from front to back, eating lunch. Near the end stood a bunch of dessert trees. Finally, a single tree held toothbrushes, toothpaste, dental floss and mouthwash. Apparently you can still get cavities in Heaven.

Then came an extremely loud "beeeep" that scared the shit out of me. It was like the time clock at the end of third shift in the factory where I work, only 100 times louder. This told me I'd visited Heaven long enough. A gold-plated time clock hung from a wall. A card made of rubies and diamonds had my name on it, and I punched out.

Immediately I woke up in an ice-fishing shack on Oconomowoc Lake, where my buddies and I were angling for panfish. They noticed I was breathing again and asked me to pass them another beer.

Cody H., Austin, Texas

Where I'm from, they say "Keep Austin Weird," but Austin isn't even in the same league of weirdness as Heaven.

I found myself in the middle of a choir singing "You Can't Always Get What You Want." Why would they sing a Rolling Stones song? Why not "Amazing Grace" or something? I wasn't able to get an answer about that, but they did move me from the sopranos to the tenors.

Next I entered the Heavenly Dinner Theater, which is like showplaces in Vegas and Branson, with comfortable chairs and perfect acoustics. The show starred ancient performers suspended in time by cosmetic surgery: Wayne Newton, Engelbert Humperdinck, Paul Anka, and one of the Beach Boys' roadies. They sang mediocre cover tunes. The Baby Boomers in the audience were thrilled, but I was bored out of my skull. Also, the dinner wasn't anything to write home about. That's typical of dinner theaters on Earth, but I didn't think they'd try to get away with it in Heaven.

Leaving the theater, I encountered the Grim Reaper on the sidewalk. He looked just like you'd expect: draped head to toe in black crepe, with a long, skeletal finger sticking out of his sleeve. I said, "Hey, bro, whassup?" and tried to give him a fist-bump in the finger, but he shouted, "You're dead now, so shut up!"

The whole experience rattled me. It didn't seem like Heaven, but it probably wasn't Hell, either, because the heat and dewpoint were comfortable. After I came back to Earth, I asked our parish priest for his opinion. He said I'd landed in Purgatory. I'm not keen about going back to Purgatory when I die for good, so I've converted to Buddhism.

Lately I'm feeling so pessimistic about life after death. I've always believed in doing the right thing, like trying to find the owner of a lost penny on the sidewalk, or joining in a standing ovation for a truly abysmal performance. But what's the point, if we won't be rewarded in the afterlife?

Ah, but that is where you are wrong. The afterlife has different Neighborhoods rewarding different lifetime achievements. It's kind of like frequent flyer points for airline travel: elite, business class, and basic. These points never expire (or so we're told; I'm still ticked off about United.)

Neighborhood 1 is reserved for people with billions of points, like Dr. Martin Luther King Jr., Abraham Lincoln, St. Joan of Arc, Clara Barton, and others who've profoundly changed our world for the better. If you're old enough to waste time reading this, you've already squandered too many years to reach Neighborhood 1.

Neighborhood 2 is for deeply flawed people who nevertheless made great contributions, like Pete Rose, former President Richard Nixon, and Ozzy Osbourne.

Neighborhood 3 is like an improved version of life on Earth. Your mortgage is paid up, and your basement doesn't smell like mildew. The ice cream in your kid's ice cream cone will never fall on the ground, even if he holds it upside down. The propane tank of your Weber grill is always full. There's no one in front of you at the pharmacy window of Walgreen's. All the pets you've ever known are there in Neighborhood 3, and somebody else cleans up after them in the litterbox or lawn.

Beyond N3, the quality of life falls dramatically. Neighborhood 4 consists of elderly people eternally griping about aches and pains they used to have before they were healed in Heaven. Neighborhood 5 includes long-winded preachers and would-be authors of children's books with bunnies and birds that talk to each other.

The remaining Neighborhoods are so bleak that you might want to stay on Earth forever. But most of us (Betty White notwithstanding) can't live forever.

So hustle now, while you've still got the chance to make Neighborhood 3. Every little thing counts. Give the waitress more than your usual 5 percent tip. Return your shopping cart to the corral instead of resting it against somebody's car. Smile at someone you despise. See you in Heaven!

84

MESSAGES FROM BEYOND THE GRAVE

Strange things have happened lately, and something tells me they're related to the recent passing of my uncle, Dirk Diggler. Sadly, I can't imagine him going to Heaven. Is he trying to tell me something?

It's quite possible. A phenomenon called After-Crisis Death Communication (AC/DC) sometimes occurs when dead people get stuck on the Highway to Hell. Desperate to avoid eternal agony, longing to ascend to Heaven (or, at the very least, return to their crummy life on Earth), they communicate with living friends and relatives in bizarre ways.

You're being targeted if you notice any of these signs:

- All the lights in your house turn on and flash "get me outta here" in Morse Code
- You receive an eBay package of dead fish wrapped in newspaper
- A telegram arrives: NOT DEAD YET (STOP) FEET ARE SMOKING (STOP) SEND LAWYERS GUNS AND MONEY
- The waiter in your favorite restaurant mistakenly brings you a platter of dead duck
- Your phone ringtone gets stuck on "Funeral March of a Marionette"

My son-in-law-in-Hell asked for lawyers, guns and money, but I can't find lawyers or gun dealers willing to venture into the afterlife. Money is my only option, so how do I send it?

Western Union offers Money Transfer Post-Mortem for a hefty fee. You must provide your recipient's name, date of death, and approximate degree of stuckness. Western Union has carriers throughout Stuckville, so desperate people can get their cash quickly.

PayPal offers a similar service within its highest fee bracket. Your recipient must be able to set up a PayPal account, which can be difficult without a corporeal presence. Once the payment goes through, it appears automatically in the recipient's bank account. Dark forces from the netherworld will access it there.

My wife is happily settled in Heaven. Every night she speaks to me in dreams, raving about Heaven's perfect weather, its Culver's restaurants on every corner, its weekly bowling tournaments, and so on. Meanwhile, I'm trapped in my crummy life with my dead-end job and the crappy winter cold and ice. How can I ask her to stop blabbing without hurting her feelings?

Asking your wife to zip it certainly would hurt her feelings, but you deserve your beauty sleep, too. Consider investing in a pair of Long-Suffering Husband UnHearing Aids™. These noise-cancelling gizmos automatically zero in on high frequencies, where wifey voices usually reside.

While most guys wear their UnHearing Aids during the day, there's no reason you can't insert them at bedtime. Set them on "internal mode" to cancel the noise that originates between your ears. Your wife doesn't seem to expect you to grunt or reply "Yes, dear," so you can slumber deeply while she gives you the daily recap.

THE FIRST <BLEEPING> WHITE HOUSE PRESS CONFERENCE OF PRESIDENT JOE PESCI

Mr. President, how did it feel on the night of the election when major news outlets declared you the winner?

It felt <bleeping> fantastic. Absolutely great. Even better than the day I became a made man. Because now I'm the made-est man on the planet. I don't answer to nobody.

Not even the voters who elected you?

As long as they back me up 100% and keep their heads down, they're fine. But if they turn on me, watch out. Watch out. Everybody in my cabinet has a shovel and a bag of lime in the trunk of his car. You know what I'm sayin'?

Mr. President, during the campaign, you declined to reveal your plans for Health and Human Services. Now that you've taken office, can you outline your position?

Yeah, I'm glad you asked that. Our new gang will help everybody. Or at least everybody who voted for me, and we have ways of finding out that information. We'll have resources for food, and drugs, and medical devices.

Could you be more specific?

Yeah, sure. The resources for food would be, like, where to get the best spaghetti Bolognese, and which restaurants have tasty lasagna, and stuff like that. When it comes to drugs — we're way ahead of the curve on that one. We've got cannabis jelly beans. We've got that insane powdered garlic everybody's snorting. Our crew has been trafficking since Prohibition, so we know what we're doing.

And medical devices, now that's really nuts. I didn't want to let the cat out of the bag during my campaign, because other gangs would love to know how we've done it, but let's just say that if you're shot full of holes like a Swiss cheese, our clinics can patch you up and get you back on the street in no time.

Mr. President, what is your position on gun control?

Gun control? Are you <bleeping> kidding me? You're asking *me* about gun control?! I just won the election on the platform of Guns For All. Were you asleep when that happened, or did you just have your head up your <bleep>? My so-called "position" on gun control is that my guys have the guns, and we're in control!

Mr. President, what about climate change?

Yeah, let's all whine about the weather. Look, I don't care about a few polar bears floating on icebergs, all right? I got better things to do. Maybe we'll send them an ocean freighter with a <bleep>load of ice cubes.

<nervous laughter among reporters>

Hey, you in the front row. Yeah, you, Poindexter. You think that's funny, huh? You think I'm funny, like a clown? Do I make you laugh? Yeah, that's it, close your notebook and sneak away. Hey, Frankie, show this guy the way out, to the Dumpster at the loading dock.

Mr. President, where did you buy the suit you're wearing?

Where did I — my suit? You're asking where I got this *suit?*

Yes, Mr. President.

Aw, for the love of — you got a lotta <bleeps>, you know that? I'll tell you, wise guy. My personal tailor in Jersey put together this custom suit for me. Look here, the shiny material, the wide lapels, the expensive buttons. Sharp, eh? Sharp-dressed man, that's me. I love that question. Thanks, man. That took guts. I'm gonna find a place for you in my cabinet. Let's put our heads together as soon as we're done with this <bleeping> media stuff.

Mr. President, what about foreign affairs? During the campaign, you made veiled threats against Canada.

Yeah, and now that I'm Mister Big Stuff, I can make unveiled threats. Everybody knows that tons of medical marijuana and other <bleep> has been coming here from across the border, but Canada hasn't paid us a dime in tariffs. We're gonna clamp down on that. Tighten the screws on those frozen <bleeps>. All right, this is getting pretty stupid. One more question and then I'm outta here.

Mr. President, do you have a message for the American people?

Yeah, I sure do. Listen up, America: four more years! Four more years or else! Four more years or <bleeping> else!

<White House Press Secretary Anthony Novato Buppo> That will be all, ladies and gentlemen. <mutters to Secret Service men> Pull him out *now.*

Four more <bleeping> years! You don't know who you're messing with, people!! Four more years!!!

DUMB HOUSEKEEPING: 10 MILLION WAYS TO COMPLICATE YOUR LIFE

There's too much to do, I hate the way I look, and I'm dreading the upcoming holiday season. Can you help?

It sounds like you need to rearrange your priorities. Here at Dumb Housekeeping magazine, it's our mission to help you simplify everything.

Let's start with facial beauty care. We recommend dozens of products you must use daily.

But that doesn't simplify things. I barely have time to apply mascara.

Trust us. After you get the hang of this routine, it takes only 90 minutes each morning. Our products are top-rated by actual celebrities, and you'll look much more polished when they're plastered all over your face. You'll even be helping the environment! Our nature-friendly facial wipes biodegrade in a few months when composted.

We live in a fifth-floor walk-up. How am I supposed to make a compost pile?

Use our Dumb and Dirty Bathtub Composting Kit, available for just
$59.99 at DumbHousekeeping. com.

**OK, well, I do need help with my hair. Sometimes it's frizzy, and some-
times it's flat.**

Chances are, you're using ordinary shampoo, conditioner and maybe
some gel. You've got to step up!

We recommend:

- Good Enough to Eat™ natural shampoo with honeycomb bits,
  powdered sugar, blackberry jam and mini marshmallows. It's free
  of parabens, seraphims, and cherubims.
- Badass™ conditioner with motor oil, Lysol, and creosote
- Rainbow Jello™ Souped-Up Hair Gel for a sleek look that also
  attracts butterflies
- Mini Cattle Prod™ Curling Iron & Child Discipline Tool (illegal in
  some states)

What about year-end holidays? I start freaking in mid-September.

September — ha! You should start in June. Get in the mood by listen-
ing to a Perry Como Christmas album and spraying your house with
pine-scented room deodorizer. You'll know you're there when your
breathing becomes shallow, your shoulders tighten, and your jaw is
clenched. As the song says, it's the most wonderful time of the year:
insane expectations, overwork, overindulgence, and endless opportunities for guilt. Our specialty!

You must make personalized gifts for everyone on your list. This
proves you're the most thoughtful, skilled and clever person they
know — because, let's face it, impressing other people is the true
spirit of the season.

This year, our advertising staff recommends a cute log-cabin kit available at Overdoit.com / holidays. Each of its 357 pieces is burnished
to a plastic sheen. After assembling the cabin, use craft paint to

personalize it with the recipient's name and zodiac sign. Make additional cabins for 50 of your closest friends.

Good. Now you're just getting started. Although the mini log cabin is cute, most of your friends will realize it's just a stocking stuffer. So here's a real gift: a rolling pin engraved with the recipient's name, address and zip code.

But who uses a rolling pin these days?

Everybody who's anybody, you big goof! Haven't you heard that old-fashioned home baking is back in style? Your giftee will either love the rolling pin or feel guilty because she stopped baking 30 years ago. Love it or loathe it — that's a win-win.

Other personalized gifts:

- Christmas ornaments shaped like any of the 50 U.S. states. Recommended for aging relatives who tend to forget where they live.
- golf balls stamped with the golfer's name. The pain of losing a ball in the rough is multiplied when someone else finds it and knows exactly who hit such a lousy drive.

Can you suggest a quick and easy main dish for the holidays?

No.

Can you suggest a difficult, strange and stressful main dish?

Yes! Heaven forbid you should settle for a traditional (borrrinnngg!) family feast. Decades from now, your guests will still be talking about this weird main course.

Eternity Roast Turkey

Active time: 21 hours

Total time: 47 hours (includes three freak-out periods)

Serves: all dinner guests who become overnight guests while waiting for the meal to be served

Ingredients

- One 14-pound turkey, cut into 26 pieces — ask your butcher to do this, and be ready to explain why you're turning a beautiful whole bird into instant leftovers
- Assorted seasonings lurking in your cupboard, especially old ones you want to use up
- 2 cups brown sugar
- 1 whole turnip
- 4 sticks butter, melted
- Jimmies (confectionery sprinkles) in your favorite color

Directions

Begin placing turkey pieces across three wire racks. Realize you have only one wire rack. Frantically phone neighbors and friends; drive across town and borrow two more.

Explain to guests that turkey is still eons away from doneness. Convert sleeper sofa to bed. Serve them eggnog spiked with absinthe.

Mix seasonings with brown sugar, using your fingers. Lick fingers frequently as a reward for running all over town to borrow wire racks. Sprinkle remaining sugar over the turkey pieces on wire racks. Place each rack over a cookie baking pan.

Attempt to refrigerate overnight. Realize there's not enough room in the fridge. Place two racks in the freezer. Set alarm to wake you twice during the night to rotate all three racks of turkey.

Wake up in a panic at dawn when your alarm goes off for the third time.

Remove turkey from refrigerator / freezer. Let stand for one hour, someplace where the cat can't get at it.

Pick cat hair off turkey pieces.

Pour toxic raw-turkey liquid from each cookie sheet down the drain.

Pat turkey with paper towel and murmur "Sorry about this."

Stare at turnip and wonder what you were thinking, since you've always hated turnips. Shove turnip down garbage disposal. Realize the drain is clogged with turkey fat; scream for your spouse to fix it. Take a sedative and lie down for 30 minutes.

Realize you should have preheated oven to 350 degrees half an hour ago. Set oven at 700 degrees to compensate.

Brush melted butter over turkey pieces with a baking brush, craft-paint brush or lightly used toothbrush.

Awaken your overnight guests and announce that it's cocktail hour. Serve leftover eggnog.

Roast turkey until a relatively clean finger inserted into the breast bone comes out with second-degree burns.

Sprinkle jimmies over all pieces of turkey so this main dish doubles as the dessert course.

And that's all there is to it. Bon appétit!

96

FLY CASTING: MAY THE FISH BE WITH YOU

Fly fishing can take your life into mystical realms, whether you've been watching "A River Runs Through It" or just need an excuse to buy some cool equipment at REI. Think of it: The adventure! The skill! The challenge of casting a lure without hooking the rear of your pants!

How can I learn fly fishing?

Many beginners take a class like Fly Casting for Klutzes — but if there are no rivers nearby, your group lessons might be held in a drainage ditch or a municipal swimming pool. And since everyone else is as clumsy as you are, those first few casts could be wildly off-target. Wear eye protection.

At the other end of the spectrum, you could hire a professional for one-on-one lessons in a pristine river in Montana. Be upfront about your status as a beginner. Nothing ticks off an elite guide more than unexpectedly hearing "Where are the flies?" and "You call that a fly? It's just a bunch of feathers and beads."

Why is fly fishing considered difficult?

Fly fishing isn't just a matter of catching a fish. Any idiot can do that in a well-stocked trout pond at a KOA campsite. Rather, fly fishing involves tricking the fish. You must cast your line back and forth, up and down, hither and yon, until the fish wonders "What the heck is going on up there?" and draws near to investigate. Then your carefully chosen fly tempts the fish into biting. That's a bingo!

It seems like there's a spiritual aspect to fly fishing. Where does that come from?

About 100,000 years ago, Primitive Man began to craft a mysterious aura around fly fishing. He hoped to convince Primitive Woman that he wasn't playing hooky when he should be hunting mastodons with other males of the clan. Rather, with great skill and cunning, he might catch a single fish. Primitive Woman could then clean, gut, and fry the fish for a delicious Friday night dinner.

As ages passed, fly fishermen elevated their sport to a spiritual plane. They weren't just standing around in dorky rubber overalls; they were communing with the river, the wind, the wilderness. They had created a level playing field with the wily fish. As President Herbert Hoover, an avid fisherman, put it: "All men are equal before fish." Or maybe he was just misquoting Lincoln's Gettysburg Address.

The lures seem so complicated. Where do I start?

Expect to be humbled while attempting to create a lure with your big clumsy man-fingers. (Ladies: it's devilishly hard to break into this sport; men hog all the best spots in the river. You might try going topless to distract them while you lay claim to a choice area.)

Flies come in all sorts of styles and colors: dry flies, wet flies, house flies, butter flies, and time flies. Imagine selecting beads approximately one millimeter wide, threading them onto string the width of a human hair, and adding feathers that float away every time you breathe. At some point, you must accept reality and buy your lures from tying experts. These fishermen have given up fishing altogether so they can tie feathers and beads 18 hours a day. They are the monks of the fly-fishing religion.

What happens if I actually catch a fish?

Nowhere is the philosophy of "catch and release" more firmly entrenched than in fly fishing. After all, you and the fish are like samurai warriors, sizing each other up, circling and parrying, perfectly matched in a battle of wits. If you're skilled enough to land your noble opponent, how could you possibly eat him? Or, even worse, how could you hire a taxidermist to stuff and polish him to display in your den? Would he do that to you? OK, maybe he would, if he could breathe on land and develop opposable thumbs. But give your fellow samurai the benefit of the doubt; maybe he would catch and release you, too.

Take a picture of your newly caught fish. Make sure your face is in the frame as well, so no one can accuse you of cribbing somebody else's photo from Google Images. Then return him gently to the stream and wish him well. With luck, you may meet again. With even better luck, that bodacious topless babe will also be fishing nearby.

TRIVIAL ACHIEVEMENTS IN HISTORY

A brief overview of monuments at the Museum of Trivial Achievement, Washington, D.C.

Which was the first monument in the museum's collection?

- Bucket, mop and Swiffer broom (bronze statue)

- Dedicated to Mary Martha Magdalene McIntyre, who single-handedly cleaned up after a major food fair in Galilee, 30 A.D.

- Artist's statement: "Historically, twelve men have been credited with the cleanup of fish and loaf fragments following outdoor lunch for 5,000. But you know how it is with guys — their definition of 'clean' is kind of loosey-goosey. So when the crowd left, Mrs. McIntyre scrubbed the lawn with a mop and sudsy water, then made a final pass with her Swiffer Sweeper. When she finished, that grass was clean enough to eat off of. It's too bad nobody ever tried to eat off it again."

Which monument represents the earliest historical event?

- Snake (rubber)

- Dedicated to Aahotep of ancient Egypt

- Artist's statement: "When Cleopatra decided to commit suicide by snake venom, do you think she caught that asp in the palace's back yard? No siree, Bob! She contacted the experts at Asps &

Adders. Ms. Aahotep, the local franchise owner, zipped right over there with a cute little asp that provided what the franchise called 'just the right bite.'"

Which was the first monument dedicated to an American citizen?

- "Dancing waters" fountain with centerpiece of charred timber

- Dedicated to Josephus M. Arnold, Pickett's Mill, Georgia (1844–1880)

- Artist's statement: "Josephus Arnold was a pioneer in residential fire-suppression devices during the Civil War. In the wake of General William Tecumseh Sherman's historic March to the Sea, during which Union soldiers burned everything in their path, Mr. Arnold went door to door — or rather, cinder pile to cinder pile — selling ceiling fire-sprinkler systems. His motto was 'Better Late Than Never.'"

What's the best monument from Europe?

- Small concrete replica of the Leaning Tower of Pisa

- Dedicated to the Rosetta family of Pisa, Italy

- Artist's statement: "For centuries after it was built, the famous building in Pisa, Italy, stood in a normal upright position. Hungry pilgrims who flocked to the so-called Pisa Tower were infuriated when they couldn't order pizza there. They threw rocks and painted graffiti on the building, prompting the landlord to hire Antonio 'Big Tony' Rosetta as a security guard. Day after day, night after night, Big Tony made an imposing figure as he leaned against the building. He eventually was replaced by his son, Bigger Tony, and then his grandson, Gargantuan Tony. All those years of Tony-pushing gave the tower its distinctive leaning structure so popular among tourists today. Ironically, there is now a pizza restaurant on the first floor."

Which monument is most popular among museum visitors?

- Marble nose, draped with paper
- Dedicated to Johannes Gutenberg (14th century), inventor of Kleenex
- Artist's statement: "Gutenberg's invention of the printing press was a pivotal moment in history, but fame didn't bring him fortune, because most people back then couldn't read. Years later, Gutenberg identified another opportunity in the paper-converting industry: disposable handkerchiefs. I'm delighted to learn that museum visitors enjoy posing for selfies beside the monument's 8-foot nostrils."

104

HAIR TODAY, GONE TOMORROW

Ladies First...

I need to find a new hair salon. Where do I begin? I'm freaking out!

You're right to be concerned. This is the most monumental decision you'll ever make. Give it more time and attention than if you were choosing a cardiac surgeon. After all, very few people ever examine the scars on your chest, but everyone notices your head.

Some resources:

- Check online reviews. Look for subject lines like "They dyed my hair green and then it fell out!!!"

- Concentrate on stylists who specialize in your kind of hair. Or, if you really hate your kind of hair, just pick a salon at random. Maybe they can nuke your head into submission.

- When you see someone with a hairstyle you like, run up to her and exclaim: "I love your hair! I want to look exactly like you!" Insist on taking a selfie with your heads close together. If she's still around after that, ask which stylist she uses.

What other services do hair salons provide besides haircuts and styling?

Let's see…perms, cornrows, base color, sparkles, Kool-Aid-inspired streaks, extensions…have we left anything out?

I've heard of salons doing "blowouts." What is that?

That's what we forgot — blowouts! Yes, blowouts. They're not just for dynamite anymore!

During a blowout, a beautician styles your hair with a round brush while blowing it dry. If that sounds like something you already do at home after shampooing, well, duh! Salons try to lure you in by calling it a "blow-dry bar" — but there's zero liquor involved, so forget that.

If you desperately want help drying your hair, you probably also want someone to help you eat lunch and take a bath. You don't need a salon, you need an attended care facility.

I'm shocked at the prices charged by decent salons. Maybe I should try one of those places with billboards all over town.

If you enjoy gambling, then yes, by all means, visit a no-frills franchise like El Cheapo Haircuts & Less. Some will do a decent job. Others leave you wishing you'd never been born. Danger signs:

- One of their stylists is standing in the parking lot, smoking a cigar and yelling into her cellphone. As her lunch break ends, she follows you into the salon and barks, "All right, let's get this over with."
- A prominent sign reads "Absolutely no refunds."
- You show them a picture of a hairstyle you like, and they laugh.
- They charge by the minute.

Desperate Hours: Home Hair Treatments

By now you've discovered that good salons are rare and expensive. Maybe you're reluctant to take out a second mortgage just to get your roots touched up. Try doing it yourself instead! It's a learning experience. You'll learn why you must pay more for someone who actually knows what they're doing.

My dog ate the instruction sheet that came with my home hair-coloring kit. Can you help?

Absolutely. They're all pretty much the same, anyway. Here's a typical form.

FAKE FAKEITY FAKE™ BRAND HAIR COLOR TREATMENT

We know you have nothing better to do, so set aside a week for this procedure.

Preview your color

First, test your color results on a small sample. Cut a strand of your hair (not in front where it's noticeable, dummy). Put on the disposable gloves included with this kit. Mix a few drops of the Fakey Color Goop with a few drops of Fakey Developer Goop, plus a squirt of whipped cream (not included). Drop the hair strand into the cream mixture. Wait 48 hours, then use a Brillo pad to scrape off the hardened mixture and check the color of your strand, which will be flecked with Brillo black.

Tips from our experts

Our laboratory tests have determined that pre-treating before coloring provides superior results compared to pre-treating after coloring. So rub the Fakey Pre-Treatment Goop on dry split ends of your hair. (If you prefer to trim the split ends instead, you must file an environmental impact statement with the EPA before throwing away these perfectly good chemicals.)

Do not color your hair if:

- you plan to attend an important event — for example, a wedding, coronation or parole hearing — in the near future.

- you are allergic to any ingredients in this kit, including boric acid, arsenic, and sparkling water.
- you are bald.

Consumer advisory per California health code #AB4822209: May contain peanuts.

If your hair has stubborn, resistant, strong-willed, pigheaded grays, extend the processing time of your root application. Like, say, 10 days.

Protect your clothing by draping a huge plastic tablecloth over your shoulders. Place a sign — **Danger: Hazardous Fumes** — on the bathroom door to warn other members of your household.

Okay, here goes nothing

Squeeze the tube of Fakey Color Goop into the bottle of Fakey Developer Goop. Hopefully you haven't thrown out the disposable gloves, because you really need them now. Place your gloved finger over the open tip of the bottle. Shake it thoroughly, and for gosh sakes don't point it at your face.

Now this is where it gets confusing. You could do a root application if you color every 6 weeks, or a full-head application if you've never colored your hair before (yeah, right). But in either case you'll end up saturating your entire head with Developer Goop. So what the heck, just go ahead and squirt that goop all over your skull, like ketchup on bratwurst. Pile your oily, smelly, toxic hair on top of your head. Then hide out in the bathroom for a couple of hours. You should have brought a book to read or something.

Rinse, rinse, rinse and rinse

Wearing those disposable gloves (you still have them, right?), bend over the sink. Run a bit of warm water over your hair and try working it into a lather, which isn't easy when your hair feels like a greased eel. Then rinse for a couple of months until all the color mixture is removed and you've polluted the water table of your entire county.

Towel-dry your hair. Rip off that horrid tablecloth. Walk around the house and see if anyone notices your new hair color. Most likely they will, because your head smells like a Superfund site.

...And Now for the Guys

My hairline is retreating. It's a classic case of male pattern baldness, and I'm only 28! What's going on?

Experts tell us that male pattern baldness has many causes:

- Lack of hair
- Thinning, skinny, anorexic hair
- Bat hair that only comes out at night
- Shy wallflower hair that hides beneath the scalp
- Hereditary baldness (poor choice of parents)

But how can I restore my usual head of hair?

Search for your hair just as you would for any lost item, like a set of keys or a Sam's Club membership card.

1. Try to recall the last time you had hair: Wedding reception? Pickup joint? Rodeo? Summiting Mt. Everest?

2. Phone this location and ask about their lost and found.

3. Turn your living quarters upside down as you search. Check logical places like the bathroom medicine cabinet or your coat pockets. If your hair's not there, search places you might have absent-mindedly set it down, like on the six-pack chilling in the fridge, the amp for your electric guitar, or the tool kit in the garage.

4. Give up. Buy a new head of hair (see toupee info, below). Bring it home and, as you begin to put it away, your previous head of hair

will turn up in that very spot. So now you have your original hair plus a spare rug for emergencies.

5. Download a Find My Hairline app for your smartphone to avoid repeating this catastrophe.

I wouldn't mind wearing a toupee if I could find one that looks natural.

We hear you. Nobody wants the helmet hair of Dean Koontz or the mafia mop of Morrie in "Goodfellas."

Here's what to do. Open Google Maps and search for "toupees / rugs / thatching near me." Shop locally in case your toupee requires multiple fitting sessions. You don't want to look more ridiculous than necessary.

Make sure their wigs are made of 100% human hair, not alpaca, otter, or African oryx. Study the fastening system. Velcro is considered the gold standard, but Elmer's Glue-All and duct tape are good choices for those on a budget.

Let the stylist know if you're athletic. They'll steer you toward hairpieces that withstand typical conditions when you run, bike, or skydive without a helmet.

Don't forget to ask about their return policy. If it's too lenient, you might be importing somebody else's cooties onto your scalp.

Finally, avoid making drastic changes. If you have just one-quarter head of greying hair now, a shock-top of bright red will be a dead giveaway. And you'll look like Ronald McDonald. If you just can't resist going for a major hair makeover, leave town for a year or two, cultivate a glowing tan, get a facelift, and upgrade your wardrobe. By the time you come back, everybody will have forgotten how your hair looked way back when.

HONEY, I SHRUNK THE TUXEDO

I accidentally ruined my favorite knit cap by washing it with the rest of the laundry. What other items can't be machine-washed?

Pillows made of "memory foam": They lose their memory of how to be pillows and turn into mushy marshmallows.

Tuxedos: Well, duh! Does Brad Pitt do his own laundry?

Anything flammable: Such as paint-soaked rags, Molotov cocktails, smoldering cigarettes, fireworks, and jalapeno peppers.

Delicate items: This includes hearing aids, contact lenses, photo scrapbooks, and souffles.

The tub of my washing machine smells like a septic tank. What's wrong?

After years of use, the innards of your washer accumulate dirt, mold, lint, and other deposits that professional home economists call "gunk." Yes, it's supremely unfair and ironic, but you need to wash your washing machine. It's best to use a self-service laundry, one of those 24-hour snakepits with buzzy fluorescent lighting and sketchy people snoozing on flimsy chairs. Choose the biggest front-loader in the place, and stuff your washer inside. Go run some errands while it churns, because the loud banging will wake up those sketchy people, who will scowl at you and demand cigarettes. When the wash cycle is finished, load your washer into the back of your pickup and let it air-dry on the way home.

Five years ago, I shoved my wedding dress in a corner just before we left on our honeymoon. Now it looks terrible. Must I take it to be dry-cleaned?

Believe it or not, you can machine-wash your wedding dress. The dress might shrink, but this gives you an excuse when some busy-body asks whether it still fits. So wash those red-wine stains, beer stains, and mystery stains out of that big white ghost, then stuff it back in the corner.

What other weird things can be machine-washed?

You can launder bills: dollars, fives, tens, hundreds, even thousand-dollar bills. Where did you think the phrase "money laundering" came from? Use strongly scented detergent to cover up lingering drug residue. Don't wash coins, though; the racket will sound like Al Capone's gang shooting up your laundry room with tommy guns.

Backpacks and lunch bags can be washed, after you've removed and eaten their contents.

You can wash your pet's cushy bed. Be sure to remove the pet first and place her someplace safe, like a bookshelf.

Can I machine-wash extremely muddy clothes?

Sure. You can also spend the next three days shoveling mud out of your washer.

How about my favorite baseball hat?

Ummm, let's see — sure, why not? Let us know how that goes.

CARSON'S FINAL ELEVEN: READ THESE WHEN YOU HAVE NOTHING BETTER TO DO

114

TOFU OR NOT TOFU? THAT IS THE QUESTION

Everybody's talking about tofu. What's the real story?

Some people hate tofu. They think it's a dense white blob that tastes like wallpaper paste, but that's unfair to wallpaper paste.

Others are big fans of tofu. They're all excited because it's made from "soy milk." OK, stop right there. Real milk is a delicious substance produced by dairy cows and goats. Soy milk isn't milk. It's not obtained by massaging the udder of a soy-mammal. It's made from raw soybeans.

Have you ever tasted raw soybeans? There is no "there" there. Just glance at any food-heat index: five-alarm habanero peppers go through the roof; soybeans dwell in the basement.

But wait — it gets worse. Soymeisters take these tasteless raw soybeans, turn them into coagulated soybean curds, and press them into solid bricks. Tofu was originally known as bean curd. At some point the health-food crowd realized that "bean curd" sounds repugnant, so they renamed it tofu. They probably hoped the term "tofu" would remind people of kung-fu, as in kung-fu fighting, where those kicks were fast as lightning.

You can find tofu in your supermarket's produce section, or maybe you won't find it, and you'll buy tasty cottage cheese instead. If you do take home a block of tofu, open the package carefully, since the soy brick is completely submerged in water. Tofu must be rinsed prior to use. Maybe that slimy brick slips from your hands and dives down the garbage disposal. Oh, darn.

The water in which the tofu resides must be changed every day, kind of like a fish tank. More opportunities for "accidental" slippage! At this point you probably feel guilty for spending good money on something you'll never eat. Be of good cheer: tofu's freshness expires after one week, and then you can throw it out with a clear conscience.

If anyone else has some stupid questions about tofu, bring 'em on.

You've missed an important point: tofu is a versatile ingredient that takes on the flavor of spices and other ingredients.
So does paper toweling, but you wouldn't throw a sheet of Bounty into your stir-fry.

You haven't mentioned how tofu can boost a weight-loss plan.
Thanks for bringing that up. Tofu can indeed help you lose weight if it kills your appetite. Or if you manage to swallow a forkful and immediately gag.

Americans need to broaden their protein choices. People in Japan have been eating tofu for centuries.
Some of them still do, but the smart ones have switched to American protein, like Big Macs and deep-fried cheese curds.

I'm looking for ways to disguise tofu, because my husband and kids won't eat anything except traditional foods.
Then they're smarter than you. But here are some wacky ideas that just might work.

- Use a paring knife to carve extra-firm tofu into the shape of a turkey. Paint it with soy sauce.

- Roll tofu into tubes, grill them on the barbecue, drench with mustard and serve with baked beans.
- Place one cup of soft tofu in your food processor. Add two cups granulated white sugar. Whip into a froth. Spread this "frosting" over a pan of brownies.

Can you provide the recipe for tofu scramble?

You're mistaken — it's not a recipe. Tofu scramble is what happens when people realize you're serving tofu, bolt from the table, and stampede out the door.

My teenage daughter turned vegetarian this year and wants tofu in place of animal protein.

Sit her down and have a nice mother-daughter chat in which you cheerfully explain who pays the mortgage, drives her to soccer practice, buys her clothes, and will be paying her college tuition. This vegetarian thing? She'll get over it.

I've heard that tofu can be cooked just like any meat, fish, or poultry. This sounds great! Can you help?

Let's be honest. You can bake tofu, fry tofu, blend tofu, fricassee tofu, skewer tofu, or saute tofu.

In the end, it's still tofu. Your taste buds know the difference; your digestive system reflexively shuts down. There's no way that gelatinous blob stays in your stomach. Keep a bucket handy.

118

MINDLESS MEDITATION

This transcript summarizes a Mindless Meditation group session, led by Ms. Woowoo Kookaburra, when the moon was in the seventh house and Jupiter aligned with Mars.

Let's all focus on our breath. As your breath moves in, silently say "In with the good air." As your breath moves out, silently say "Out with the bad."

In with the good air, out with the bad. In with the good air, out with the bad.

Hey, I said *silently!* And turn off those cellphones!

Imagine your breath moving in and out of your heart… in and out of your liver…in and out of your belly button.

All right, now, come back to the real world and focus your attention on me. Who would like to share their experience of mindlessness?

Sucker 1: I felt my hands and feet tingling.

That's a common reaction. Your psychic energy is flowing into the wall outlets. In fact, whenever we hold workshops, the venue gives us an energy rebate.

Sucker 2: I didn't feel anything.

That's a common reaction. You must look deeper. How do your kidneys feel? Your bladder? Your prostate?

I don't have a prostate. I'm a woman.

That's a common response. Try to imagine, for the sake of argument, how your prostate would feel if you had one.

I do feel my bladder. It's full. I need to use the restroom.

You can't leave this sacred space until we've all spoken our truth. Your departure would distort the energy field.

Who else has an experience to share?

Sucker 3: I feel like I've been hit by a concrete-mixer truck.

That's a common symptom. You're making concrete progress.

Sucker 4: My earlobes tingled.

That's a common symptom. The earlobes are connected to the frontal lobes of the brain. Do you wear pierced earrings?

I do, and my skin is allergic to nickel. I need to remove these cheap earrings I bought yesterday.

No, don't do that! Keep those earlobes tingling to generate more energy.

Sucker 5: I felt like I was in a giant whirlpool, circling the drain.

That's a common feeling. Do you still have a pulse? Anyone else with this symptom? Raise your hand, so we know what to tell the 911 dispatcher.

Sucker 6: I saw color, swirling and splashing.

That's a common experience. Any particular color?

Sherwin Williams SW 6385, Dover White. That's the only color my landlord lets me use on the walls.

Dover White is a common color. The universe is in agreement with your soul.

Sucker 7: I saw a black-and-white houndstooth pattern.

Sucker 8: I saw pink polka dots.

Sucker 9: I saw tangerine trees and marmalade skies.

These are all common experiences! In the mindless state, many colors and patterns appear. Some are muddy, some are bright. Sometimes they burst like fireworks — the good ones that cost $300 each — and sometimes they drip down the wall of your mind's eye like a rotten tomato thrown at a lame karaoke singer.

Sucker 10: Is there anything that's *not* "common" in your dumb interpretations?

It's not common for us to refund your money. In fact, it never happens. One of my assistants will show you out.

FRIENDS DON'T LET FRIENDS LINE DANCE: THREE WARNING SIGNS OF STEP-ADDICTION

Warning Sign 1: Making Excuses

A close friend said she's worried that my line dancing is getting out of control. She's overreacting, right? — *Patsy Line*

Unfortunately, your friend is probably correct. By the time other people notice your condition, you're already a step-aholic.

But I need the exercise.

Yeah, we've heard that one before. You could get more exercise walking out of the shower and toweling yourself dry.

Anyway, all my friends do it.

So all your friends are step-aholics too.

Even better, my husband covers the housework for me when I'm out line dancing.

He's an enabler.

Warning Sign 2: Stepping Out of Bounds

I figure it only counts when I'm dancing in class, so I've been stepping on my own more often. — *Jabba the Hoot*

No, just the opposite: your step-aholism has gotten worse. Have you ever line-danced in the supermarket aisle?

Well, yes. Barry Manilow was singing "Mandy," and I couldn't help myself.

That song doesn't even have a danceable beat.

I admit it wasn't one of my better routines.

Where else have you experienced this "couldn't help myself"?

Last week I did the Electric Slide while waiting in line at the Department of Motor Vehicles.

Oh, for pity's sake. Don't you realize the trauma you inflicted on everyone else? Waiting for hours at the DMV *and* getting stuck near a line dancer? Those poor people.

They offered to let me move to the front, but I wasn't done dancing yet.

I'm surprised they didn't take up a collection to pay you off.

They did, but no amount of money could come between me and my line dancing.

Bingo! Step-aholic!

Warning Sign 3: Denial

I'm not like those other line dancers. I can stop anytime I want. — *Dr. NoNoNoooo*

When was the last time you stopped?

On the Fourth of July, when the cops pulled me out of a parade for dancing alongside our high-school marching band playing "Wooly Bully."

We don't consider that stopping anytime you want.

I suddenly stopped as they shoved me into the back seat of a squad car.

Have you experienced other symptoms of advanced step-aholism? Memory loss, for instance?

No, I'm sure I'd remember if that happened.

The legal briefs in yesterday's paper said you danced for nearly an hour on Walgreen's roof before they talked you down.

What?! I never did that!

I rest my case.

VARIETY IS THE LIFE OF SPICE

Courtesy of Twice the Spice Up Your Nose, LLC

Lately I've been cooking from scratch more often. Which seasonings should I have on hand?

The following are essential, in our opinion. You may not have heard of them; you might never see a recipe that calls for them; but we sell them, so you'd better stock up.

Arrowroot powder provides a thickening agent for sauces, stews and latex paint. Arrowroot was originally used by native tribes to heal poison-arrow wounds; today it comes in handy during heated family arguments.

Caraway seeds have fans all over the world, who use them in Leyden cheese, madeira cake, and sauerkraut — so if you don't like the taste of caraway, you're a provincial rube. But you should keep some on hand anyway in case random strangers from the Netherlands, England, or Germany show up unexpectedly in your dining room. Scandinavians put caraway to its best use in aquavit, an alcoholic beverage that tastes like rye bread…or maybe that's not such a great idea, either. OK, we officially excuse you from buying caraway seeds.

Blue cheese is famously smelly; it harbors the same bacteria that produce foot odor. Add a concentrated dose of repellence to your seasoning rack with our blue cheese powder. When you're sick and tired of those unwelcome Dutch, English and German guests who dropped in for caraway seeds, just open a container of this stink bomb and wave it around.

Coriander seeds have distinct "nutty" and "peppery" notes that remind us of Great-Aunt Gertrude, who used to chase us around the garden with her bumbershoot. If you're aiming to develop an eccentric personality, add 1 tablespoon of coriander to your afternoon tea.

Curry was first imported to England in the 1600s by the British East India Company. Today it remains an essential flavoring in curries. Well, duh!

Fennel is associated with Sicilian cuisine. When those heated family arguments (see arrowroot, above) turn into lifelong blood feuds, fennel just might save your life. Don Vito Corleone used it daily, and he survived five gunshot wounds in an assassination attempt, so there you go.

How do you like your **garlic**? Whether roasted, chopped, granulated or minced, we've got the goods to weaponize your garlic breath for up to 24 hours. Choose your favorite formulation to make tasty garlic toast, garlic schaum torte, and garlic smoothies.

Ginger is the sucker-punch of spices. Sounds so innocent. Looks so mellow-yellow and mild. But massive quantities of ginger in tea, soup, or casserole will transform your guests into whirling dervishes, desperate for something, *anything* to quench the fire on their tongues. Nyah-ha-ha!

Horseradish powder will put hair on your chest. Women, don't say we didn't warn you. Horseradish is also prized as a sinus purge, so set the table with your biggest handkerchiefs.

Mace comes in handy when you're forced to walk through a bad neighborhood after dark. If you still have mace left over when you get home, pair it with meatballs and mothballs. Fun fact: mace is the seed covering of a nutmeg. And you thought your job was bad! Imagine cracking nutmegs all day long with your bare fingernails.

If only you had the strength of a **mustard seed,** you could attain the Kingdom of Heaven and slather mustard all over an eternal bratwurst.

Munch a spoonful of **black sesame seeds**, which stick to your teeth. You can tell people you've been snacking on Iranian Beluga caviar ($34,500 per kilogram).

Barbecuing over a mesquite-wood fire may sound like fun, but soon you'd tire of getting smoke in your eyes while warding off hungry coyotes. Skip the southwestern hassles by adding our **mesquite smoke powder** to all your favorite meats, including coyote and kangaroo.

Turmeric is today's wonder spice. Buy it now; consume it voraciously for a while. Then let it get shoved to the back of your spice cabinet. Someday you'll notice the bottle and wonder why you ever fell for the myth that it's a cure-all for mood and memory. Or maybe you won't remember buying it at all. A memory aid? What's that?

KIND OF A DRAG

Back in the '60s, I really liked the song "Kind of a Drag" by the Buckinghams. Did they ever record a follow-up? Maybe something like "Kind of Feeling Better Now"?

No, because that would be Kind of a Dumb Song. But the understatement is fascinating: The singer's girlfriend doesn't love him anymore. He knows she's cheating on him. Yet it's only "kind of a drag."

What if other people had that laid-back attitude? How would history be different?

I don't get what you're driving at.

Suppose that near the end of World War II, Adolf Hitler had said, "It's kind of a drag when your U-boat fleet is decimated, you're fighting on two fronts, the Allies are hammering your infantry, and Eva isn't sure she wants to go through with this suicide thing." Except he'd say it in German, of course.

That's doesn't sound like —

Or what if Vincent van Gogh said, "It's kind of a drag to live in poverty because nobody buys your artwork and you only have enough money for a loaf of bread or a paintbrush, but not both, and you know you're ahead of your time and people won't appreciate your genius until it's too late, so you cut off your ear and that just makes things worse because the styptic pencil doesn't work and now the knife is bloody so you wouldn't use it on bread even if you could afford bread."

But that's not a laid-back attitude.

OK, bad example, but we could all try to be more self-aware. Remember that video of "Pinky the adoptable cat"? That guy could say, "It's kind of a drag when you're holding a cat that goes ballistic and winds his leash around your leg, and you scream as he sinks his teeth into your hamstring, and the whole mess goes viral."

Hey, I saw that! Pinky made that guy famous.
And he'd better be cool with it, because the video will circulate till the end of time.

So it's mainly about accepting bad things that happen to you?
Come to think of it, maybe it's seeing bad things happen to other people, too. Like the radio announcer in 1937 watching the airship *Hindenburg* exploding: "It's burst into flames! It's on fire…and it's crashing! It's a mass of smoking wreckage. Oh, the humanity! This is the worst thing I've ever witnessed, ladies and gentlemen. Well, maybe not the worst thing. But it's truly, truly kind of a drag."

Wow. This is so Zen-like. If you could honestly view terrible things as just "kind of a drag," you'd reach the highest plane of detachment. Nothing would disturb your inner peace. Hey, I could write a book about this, and create a website! I'd be a celebrity! I'd do TED Talks… appear on talk shows…

That sounds like Kind of a Bore.
Oh, shut up.

LOVE UNREQUITED? DON'T GET SO EXCITED

By guest columnist Maureen Goodluck

Dear Lady Goodluck: So I met this hot chick, she calls herself Juliet. We were both crazy in love right away when we first seen each other. But then we started talking, and she totally disrespected me. I think it's 'cause our families don't get along real good, like they poison each other's food and stuff like that. How can I get Juliet to be totally into me? — *Romeo in fair Verona*

Dear Romeo: Juliet is turned off by the way you speak, and no wonder. You sound like a moron. A sweet maiden like Juliet deserves to be wooed with poetic prose. These examples will get you started:

> *But, soft! what light through yonder window breaks?*
> *It is the east, and Juliet is the sun.*

And:

> *See how she leans her cheek upon her hand!*
> *O, that I were a glove upon that hand,*
> *That I might touch that cheek!*

Practice those lines until you can say them without being mistaken for a dunce. Good luck!

Dear Maureen: 14 years, 3 months and 10 days after breaking up with my hypercritical boyfriend, I'm ready to move on. Can you give me some practical tips? — *Sloth in Seattle*

Dear Sloth: Here are helpful ways to get over a crush.

Stop interacting

Block their number on your cellphone. Avoid places where you used to meet. Build a brick wall around their house so you won't see them in an unguarded moment. Put out a warrant for their arrest on the basis of "alienation of affection."

Learn from your mistakes

What subtle signs should you have noticed early on? For instance, weird hobbies like axe-throwing. Or giving you a strip of beef jerky for Valentine's Day. Or tattoos all over their nose. Framing these bad qualities as "things to avoid next time" resets your outlook toward the future.

Stay busy with fun activities

Consider reviving long-ago passions like sculpting Play-Doh or climbing the wood fort at the playground. Or take up intriguing new pastimes like pole dancing; breeding and showing Weimaraners; or chewing tobacco.

Concentrate on your strengths

Now that you've liberated yourself from Mr. Grumpy Pants, practice positive self-talk: "I'm brilliant. I'm funny. I can play four chords on the ukulele. I know all the words to the Pythons' Lumberjack Song. And I smell pretty good after a shower."

And, since it took you more than 14 years (gaakk!) to start moving on from this abyss, allow yourself plenty of time (another 14 years?) to return to whatever "normal" means to you. Good luck!

Dear Ms. Goodluck: I've been dating "Lenny" for about a year. Recently, many things about him started getting on my nerves. He's lazy and out of shape, he's got terrible breath, his comb-over is ridiculously fake, and he smacks his lips every time he eats. I was about to break up with Lenny when *he* broke up with *me!* I'm so ticked off that I can't think straight. Do you have any mind games to help me get over this? — *He's Got a Lotta Nerve*

Dear Nerve: Getting over any breakup just takes time. (Although I hope it doesn't take you 14 years like it did with "Sloth in Seattle." Sheesh.) Continue focusing on Lenny's bad qualities — in particular, the comb-over. Do you have any photographs of your boyfriend standing outdoors when it's windy? Post them on your refrigerator and your bathroom mirror. Then reinforce your scorn by letting the following song run through your mind all day long. Good luck!

When Your Lover's Hair Flips Over
(Tune: "What Do You Do When a Love Affair Is Over?")

His comb-over hair makes people stare
It's a source of much amusement
See, they look at me, contemptuously,
Saying, girl you oughta lose him
Now each windy day picks up his hair
*   and blows it the wrong way*
What am I to do
What can you do, when your lover's hair flips over?

All plastered with gel, those skinny strands
Always look so dark and greasy
Still, gel doesn't help, just makes it worse
When the weather turns this breezy

I'll try not to smile, though it looks like his scalp
*   is standing at attention*
What else can I do
What can you do, when your lover's hair flips over?

SUBURBAN LEGENDS: BECAUSE URBAN LEGENDS AREN'T ALREADY DUMB ENOUGH

Q. We heard that huge alligators live in the New York City sewage system. People on vacation in Miami brought live baby gators back home to NYC, then dumped them down the sewer drains when they got too big. My friend Ed Norton swears this is true.

A. It's only partially true. New York's alligators hate winter, so they migrate to the Florida panhandle in November and return to the Big Apple in March. But Miami — now, that's a different story! Miami's sewage system is so crowded with alligators that there's a lottery system for reptile residency. The city is also building bunkers for homeless gators so they don't harass drug dealers and gang members.

Q. My Uncle Hector was ambushed and knocked unconscious while riding his Segway down the alley. When he woke up, he was missing his liver. Someone had surgically removed it for transplantation. How can I help him?

A. It wasn't his liver; it was his bladder. And by the time we contacted Hector, he'd been knocked out again, and the bladder was back in place. Keep in mind that agencies like Organs 'R' Us "borrow" bladders for wealthy patrons of the arts. The extra urine capacity enables them to watch a lengthy live performance without a bathroom break. As an example: the "Conveyor-Belt Suite" by minimalist composer Philip Glass clocks in at 6 hours, or as long as 7 hours when the conductor falls asleep at the podium. Next time Uncle Hector loses his bladder, check the performing arts schedule of your community. Most symphonies run for just one weekend. Advise Uncle Hector to be patient.

Q. A friend warned me not to reach into the coin-return slots of public payphones because drug users place hypodermic needles in there to spread HIV. How can I protect myself?

A. Suburban legend! Payphones no longer exist; that should have tipped you off (duh). But there is a grain of truth to this one. Deliberate stabbings with infected needles can occur during meet-and-greets with politicians, so when someone from a hostile political party visits your neighborhood, stay indoors. If your job requires you to greet them in person, catch them off-guard with a bear hug.

Q. I've read that this urban legend is partially true: Coca-Cola once contained trace amounts of cocaine.

A. We don't know whether or not that's true, but cocaine has tons of Coca-Cola in it. No wonder it's so addictive.

Q. If I swallow watermelon seeds, will a watermelon grow in my stomach?

A. No, but if you swallow enough junk food, pretty soon your stomach will look like a watermelon.

Q. What about the "blue star tattoo" legend? It claims that LSD tabs are given to children as lick-and-stick temporary tattoos.

A. Really? Where can we get these?

Q. This one seriously creeps me out: If you listen to the Beach Boys' song "Barber Ann" six times in a row, Barber Ann will appear and slit your throat with a straight razor.

A. That's BARBARA Ann, you idiot!

Q. Years ago I heard that Paul McCartney of the Beatles died and was replaced by a lookalike.

A. Not true. However, we do know that Elvis Presley is still alive in the working-class city of Cudahy, Wisconsin. He lives in the basement of an old Polish flat and works the third shift at Ladish. Every day after work, he chugs a shot and a beer with friends at the corner tavern. We swear this is true. Cross our hearts and hope to die.

NOT ALL SEQUELS ARE CREATED EQUAL

I recall that Leonard Nimoy of "Star Trek" released an autobiography called *I Am Not Spock*. Didn't he also write a sequel?

Yes. In fact, he wrote two sequels. After *I Am Not Spock* sold well, Nimoy was emboldened to release *Okay, I Am Spock (When I'm Trying To Sell Autobiographies)*. His third book — the "threequel," you might say — was *As Spocky As I Wanna Be*. Although Nimoy has passed away, we've heard rumors that a fourth book is being transcribed during séances with a spiritual medium.

Nichelle Nichols of "Star Trek" played Lt. Uhura and later released her autobiography, *Beyond Uhura*. Did she publish a sequel, too?

No. Nichols, who is African American, also wrote *How I Became the 1,000th Woman to Kiss White Actor William Shatner,* but the five-page manuscript failed to stir interest from publishers.

As for William Shatner: he was already typecast as Captain Kirk when "Star Trek" was cancelled in 1969. How bad was it, and how did he get back into sequels?

Being pigeonholed as Captain Kirk took Shatner out of the running for coveted film roles as Pope Pius II, Tarzan, and Aretha Franklin. For years, Shatner was reduced to doing TV commercials for Hostess Twinkies, Handi-Wipes, Charmin toilet tissue and Goodyear tires.

Then, one day, producers pulling together the first "Star Trek" feature film saw Shatner's outstanding performance in a 30-second spot for Crisco Shortening, and the rest is history.

Is getting typecast really so bad? I loved the "Lassie" TV show and the two Lassie movies.

Lassie certainly had a lock on the collie franchise, and for years those roles were her bread and butter — or rather, her kibble and Milk Bones. But at some point, viewers showed signs of collie fatigue. Their attention moved to other dogs ("Rin Tin Tin"), talking horses ("Mr. Ed"), and benevolent witches ("Bewitched"). The low point occurred with the TV series "My Mother the Car," which torpedoed the careers of Jerry Van Dyke and the antique touring car in the title role. When the series was cancelled after one season, Mother-Car suffered a nervous breakdown and was committed to a scrap yard in Pasadena.

Which other actors have been typecast?

After years as nerdy Deputy Barney Fife in "The Andy Griffith Show," Don Knotts starred as a nerdy fish in "The Incredible Mr. Limpet" and a nerdy vampire in "Dracula Does Mayberry." Surprisingly, Knotts was a nerd in real life, too. Insider tip: Don Knotts and Mick Jagger of the Rolling Stones were separated at birth. Check out their lips.

Ralph Macchio traded on his popularity in "The Karate Kid" with "The Karate Kid Marries and Moves to the Suburbs" and "The Karate Kid Has a Midlife Crisis." A third sequel, "The Karate Kid Applies for Social Security," is in development.

The Three Stooges never could break out of playing three stooges. Their agent shopped around a few serious dramatic concepts like "We Three Kings of Orient Are," but nothing ever clicked. They spent their final years in a Hollywood assisted-living residence, starting pie fights, turning leaky faucets into geysers, and breaking plates over each other's heads.

What are the best movie sequels of the past two decades?

Everyone's taste is different, of course, but you can't go wrong with the following:

- "There Will Be Blood" spawned "There Will Be Bloodstains" and "There Will Be Spray 'N Wash Laundry Stain Stick."

- "Black Swan" bequeathed "Black Sheep," "Black Eye," "Blacktop" and "Blackbird Singing in the Dead of Niiiiiight."

- The lone sequel to "Inglourious Basterds" was "Inglorious Bastards: The Proofreader's Cut."

- "Tinker Tailor Soldier Spy" led to "Cashier, Bagger, Butcher and Produce Guy."

- "The Pianist" had dozens of sequels, including "The Trombonist," "The Tubist" and "The Drummer Who Makes Our Choir Sound Like a Lounge Act."

QUANTUM PHYSICS MADE EASY

I've been feeling discouraged about my social life. My sister mentioned that quantum physics could help. What the heck is she talking about?

It's quite possible that quantum physics is involved. What's wrong with your social life?

Whenever my husband and I are out with other people, he gets all the attention. It's ridiculous.

Like what?

Yesterday I was wearing my outrageous neon-purple scarf, but our friends complimented him on his dirty old Winn-Dixie ball cap.

Interesting. What about conversations? Do they pay attention to you?

That's another thing! We were talking about "The Beverly Hillbillies," and I made a funny remark that fell flat. Half a minute later, one of the guys said exactly the same thing, and everybody laughed!

Oh, so it's not just your husband — it's all the men, right?

That's true. Men are the 800-pound gorillas in our crowd. All of us ladies are no-see-ums.

Have you considered a sex-change operation?

I'm pretty sure my insurance won't cover it.

OK, then, let's deal with your problem from a quantum-physics perspective.

You're suffering from Invisible Woman Syndrome. A disruption in the space/time continuum turns you into a one-dimensional object whenever men are around. You're barely a shadow, about 2 millimeters wide.

What's more, when you speak, the sound emerges as subliminal particles, which explains why that guy thought your joke came from his own brain.

The first law of quantum physics says that everything in the universe is made of waves, particles or Legos. In your case, the men are making waves, and the Invisible Women particles get bumped aside.

It sounds like we need to be Legos.

Yes, but you have to be careful about this. If children are around, they might turn you into a castle and play war games with your private blocks.

Thanks for the tip. So how can I and my Invisible Women friends become Legos?

You must find a particle accelerator that's accepting new clients, and wait for their enrollment window. They'll also require a psych evaluation to determine whether you have any mental blocks about becoming…er, blocks.

Anything else I should know?

After you leave a group of men, you'll gradually return to human form. Check yourself once you get home (a full-length mirror in the garage works well) to make sure you're free of any loose Legos. If those Legos drop on the carpet and get stepped on by someone's bare foot, you'll both feel the pain.

KEN DON'T GET NO RESPECT

I've noticed through the years that Mattel's Barbie doll keeps climbing the career ladder, while her boyfriend Ken has hit the glass ceiling.

You're right. Barbie has been transformed into an esteemed diplomat, a neurosurgeon, and Mother Teresa. Meanwhile, Ken has become a taxi driver, restaurant busboy, sewage treatment plant inspector, and prisoner intake officer. And then there's Barbie's sister, Skipper, whose career has leapfrogged over Ken's even though she's way younger and (some say) dumber.

What does this mean for Ken's career prospects?

There will always be little girls willing to bop-bop-bop around with Ken like the standard plaything he is. But his roles are heading to the bottom of the barrel. Here are some likely marketing schemes as Mattel expands the Barbie franchise.

Netflix: "The Crown IV": Queen Elizabeth II Barbie, Princess Margaret Skipper, and royal horse carriage manure shoveler Ken

Amazon original series: "Gilligan's Island II": Ginger Barbie, Gilligan Ken, and Skipper Skipper

"Gone with the Wind": Barbie Scarlett, Skipper Melanie Wilkes, and Prissy Ken (in drag)

"Jaws": Police chief Barbie Brody, marine biologist Skipper Hooper, and Ken Bruce the shark

"The Wizard of Oz": Barbie Dorothy, Skipper The Wizard, and flying monkey Ken

Branded merchandise for adults: The Barbie Evening Wear Collection, Skipper Tween Fashions, and Ken Compression Socks

Health and beauty products: Barbie lash extensions, Skipper sunscreen, and Ken Preparation H

ASK THE MAGIC 8-BALL

Would my tongue really get stuck on a frosty metal pole?
Try it and see.

Who is buried in Grant's tomb?
Somebody named Grant.

Is that a V-2 rocket I hear overhead?
You're in the wrong century.

I've noticed you often reply "My sources say yes" or "My sources say no." Is that because you don't know the answer?
My sources say get lost.

My boyfriend says I'm too impatient. Is that true?
Reply hazy, try again.

Am I too impatient?
Ask again later.

AM I IMPATIENT?!
Yes, definitely.

How long will I live?
Better not tell you now.

I bought an abacus at a yard sale. Is it worth using?

Don't count on it.

Should I stop drinking 5-Hour Energy?

Reply hazy, stop shaking me.

Can't you ever give one-word answers?

My reply is no.

The End

ABOUT THE AUTHOR

LEAH CARSON divides her time between Wisconsin, Florida, Colorado, Wyoming and Netflix. Personal influences include Mad magazine, The Three Stooges, Monty Python, "Airplane!" and the voices in her head.

She enjoys reading, especially books on home decorating, World War II, and home decorating during World War II — but books filled with misspellings and grammatical errors make her eyes roll so far that someday they'll get stuck there. Her heroes have always been cowboys, and they still are, it seems.

Leah's previous works (you knew this was coming, right?) include *Arts and Crap, For Pets' Sake, White Lace and Panic, Desperately Seeking Sanity,* and *Gimme Shelter* — available on Kindle at Amazon for just 99 cents each. Also at Amazon in paperback: *Fifty Shades of BenGay, The Lord of the Wrinkles,* and *Da Vinny Code.*

One more thing: check out her weird merchandise at www.carsonmania.com. You'll wonder how you lived this long without a dog-themed "To lick or not to lick" dishwasher magnet.

www.carsonmania.com

www.ingramcontent.com/pod-product-compliance
Lightning Source LLC
Chambersburg PA
CBHW061725020426
42331CB00006B/1094